Teaching Strategies
for the
Online College
Classroom

A Collection of Articles for Faculty

MAGNA

Madison, Wisconsin

Magna Publications
2718 Dryden Drive
Madison, WI 53704
Magnapubs.com

Contents

Foreword

by Deidre Price

Have you ever wanted to improve your online teaching but you weren't sure where to start?

In *Teaching Strategies for the Online College Classroom,* instructors will learn best practices from other instructors who know how to repair, develop, and enhance online courses. From faculty bios to gamification, from faculty presence to student retention, this text offers accessible, practical tools to improve online courses from the first welcome message to the final exam.

In my work with online instructors, I've discovered a few common themes:

- Most online instructors want to provide quality instruction to their students.
- Most online instructors think they're doing a satisfactory job, even if they are unfamiliar with best practices for online teaching.
- Many online instructors have never taken an online course themselves, not even a bad one, so they often lack a reference point for what students might experience or what could be done well in their classrooms.
- Most instructors are willing to invest more time and energy in their online classrooms, but they encounter roadblocks that prevent them from improving their online teaching.

- Instructors learn best from other instructors.

Overall, these instructors are eager to improve their classrooms to enhance students' educational experience, and they would—if only they could identify the weaknesses, learn ways to strengthen their courses in these areas, and access and manage the tools to help accomplish these goals.

In my work with online students, I see just as many common themes:

- Online students want to produce quality work and do well in their classes.
- Most online students hope they're doing a satisfactory job but feel less sure of themselves in online classrooms than in face-to-face ones.
- Many online students are first-time students or first-time online students, but online instructors often assume experience, leaving gaps in instructions, leaving students feeling lost or confused.
- Most students are willing to invest more time and energy in their online classes, but they encounter roadblocks—life, technical, or otherwise—that prevent them from succeeding.
- Students can learn from peer-to-peer interactions.

Overall, these students want what instructors want: an environment that is communicative, participative, interactive—and just plain *active*. They want authenticity and transparency: a real, live, messy learning community where the room feels real and students come together to learn alongside one another, guided by an instructor who is present, engaged, accessible, and approachable—just as they would be given inside the face-to-face classroom.

Teaching Strategies for the Online College Classroom addresses these students' needs by providing instructors a range of ways to connect with and engage students in the online environment, and the approaches are as varied as the instructors who are sharing their experiences. In "The Start of a Successful Semester," instructors share ideas for new ways to welcome students to the online classroom, how to engage students with orientation materials, ideas for using video early in the course, and ways to establish instructor presence.

"Building Rapport with Students" is devoted to practical strategies for building learning communities in online classrooms. This section offers ideas for how to use faculty bios well in online classrooms, how to add social media as a way to engage and interact with online students, how to scaffold learning, and how to build motivation in online learners.

"Managing Challenging Behavior" addresses the problems all instructors face with classroom management, which often requires creative solutions in online environments. Subjects in this chapter range from civility to preparation in the online classroom, including discussions of academic honesty policies and procedures, ways to engage all types of students, and ideas for time management in online classrooms.

In "Strategies for Student Engagement," the writers offer ways to engage students with critical thinking and creativity. They focus on methods to improve retention and student success in online learning. The chapter also offers ways to incorporate flipped classrooms and learning logs, as well as how to enhance online discussions and implement continuous assessments.

Compiled to address instructors' needs as they build courses to meet and exceed students' expectations, *Teaching Strategies for the Online College Classroom* is an essential collection of articles and presentations that equips instructors at all experience levels with the tools to make their online classrooms work best for them and their students. It is a book I wish every online instructor would read cover to cover and then keep on hand as a reference and reminder to raise the bar and keep challenging ourselves to become better instructors who create environments where students love to learn.

Whether you're a new instructor just entering online education or you're the experienced instructor seeking a master class, this book will engage you, encourage you, and equip you.

Let's begin.

Deidre Price, PhD
Northwest Florida State College

CHAPTER 1

•

The Start of a Successful Semester

Methods for Welcoming Students to Your Course

by John Orlando, Northcentral University

Students in an online course can feel detached from the instructor and one another, so one of the most important things an online faculty member can do is send each student a welcome message. Welcoming students will kick off the learning relationship, and pay dividends in the form of better participation and performance down the line. There are a variety of ways to do it.

Welcome letter

A simple letter is the easiest way to welcome students. But remember that this should not just repeat what is in the syllabus. The point is to reach each student on a personal level.

Start by talking about why the course is relevant. Students are not interested in what is not relevant to them, so talk about how the course contributes to students' growth. If it's a "soft skills" course, like English, explain how these skills will benefit students in their future work and other endeavors. This demonstrates that you are sincerely interested in your students' growth, which will help motivate them to succeed.

Next, talk about your own teaching philosophy. Do you believe that much of learning comes from discussion with others? Then that explains why discussion is an important part of the course. What are the purposes of the assignments and other material? Explain why you are doing things and students will be more likely to look at the course as a learning experience, not just a way to satisfy a requirement.

The welcome letter is also an opportunity to head off any common problems that students encounter in the course. If students often have trouble getting organized for a group assignment, highlight this as a common problem and explain how to avoid it. These warnings based on experience will resonate far more than simply listing requirements and deadlines.

Make sure to talk about yourself. Unfortunately, faculty tend to turn to their CVs when talking about themselves. But students do not care about what their teachers publish. Talk about other things that are interesting about you and your experiences. For instance, what got you interested in your subject? Students remember the stories that humanize us to others. Also make sure to mention some personal information. I was married on a 100-mile bicycle ride, which always gets people's attention. This willingness to share a bit about yourself demonstrates your interest in connecting with students, which can only help make them feel more at ease and willing to come to you with problems.

Finally, be sure to invite students to contact you. Faculty are obligated to list their office hours on the syllabus, but it is well known that some faculty really do not want to be bothered by students showing up during that time. Make it clear that you are there to help students and invite them to reach out to you when they have a problem.

Welcome call

Many online courses require faculty to make a welcome call to each student before the course. Whereas the welcome letter is an opportunity to talk, the welcome call is more of an opportunity to listen. Skype video calling is an ideal way to make these calls, as seeing the other person often creates instant bonds.

Start by asking students about their backgrounds: Where are they from, what degree programs are they studying, do they have previous experience with online education, what are their educational goals, etc.? Then move on to more probing questions. For instance, many students come ill-prepared to be successful online learners, so asking about their preparation can head off problems later on. Do students have schedules with times blocked off during the week to do coursework? It is easy to fall behind in an online course where you do not have the schedule of a MWF 9–10 a.m. lecture imposing a structure on your day. Without this exterior structure, some students have difficulty budgeting time for class work, which is one of the most common reasons for failure in an online course.

Also ask students about their study habits. Another common cause of student failure is not knowing how to study. You can ask students how they read academic work, making suggestions for improvement. You can also talk about how you read academic work. Modeling good practice is a powerful teaching tool, and something we don't do enough of.

Another good topic is students' strengths and weaknesses. We all have academic strengths and weaknesses, yet this topic is rarely discussed, which can lead students to feeling that only they are having trouble with certain types of material. Hearing students' strengths and weaknesses will better prepare you to help them when they hand in work. Plus, merely showing interest in students will help them feel comfortable reaching out for help.

Also make sure that students understand that they are part of an academic community as participants in the course. Online learning is a fundamentally social process, and interactions with others are an important part of the learning environment. While most students seem to come out of their shells in an online discussion, it is still helpful to emphasize the importance of discussion in the course to draw them into the conversations.

Finally, make notes on the call. These notes will be valuable during the course, helping you understand how you should guide students and what might be the sources of any performance problems. You might bring up a topic that you'll discuss later on in the course to show how it connects to an issue that a student is having. This will help put performance in context, and provide the self-reflection that is a key to growth.

Video welcome

Perhaps the best demonstration of your willingness to reach students on a personal level is a video welcome. A short video about the course or yourself will humanize you to the students. These videos are easy to make with a webcam, and can be uploaded to YouTube, Vimeo, or similar services for students to watch on their own. Here is an example of a video welcome for a faculty development course that I teach, as well as some rules for making engaging video welcomes: *http://bit.ly/1DBQjOV.*

Make sure to start your online course with a welcome. The time you devote to it will more than pay for itself in smoother sailing during the course.

Reprinted from *Online Classroom*, May 2014.

The Right Way to Start Your Teaching

by John Orlando, Northcentral University

If you want to lose your audience's attention right off the bat, be it at a conference or in a classroom, here's a tip: start by outlining what you will cover. "Today I will cover these eight points…" By the time the sentence is out of your mouth, your audience has mentally checked out. They are either on their cell phones or, if they are more courteous, thinking of something else while practicing yawning with their mouths shut. Plus, nobody actually remembers that outline during the presentation—it's a waste of time.

One of the reasons we find TED Talks so compelling is that speakers are coached to never start with an outline of their topic. Instead, they begin by grabbing their audience's attention. Dan Pink's famous talk on motivation starts with the words "I have a confession to make. In a fit of youthful enthusiasm, I went to law school." Now I want to know where the story is going, so you have my attention. One by Ann Zaccardy begins with the question, "Do you think you're smart?" Try that opening on students someday.

Most teachers make the mistake of beginning their teaching modules with an outline of the topics they will cover. That is the worst way to start. Teaching is fundamentally about communicating, not covering content, and communication begins with getting your listeners psychologically invested in what you have to say. If you don't get them invested at the very beginning, nothing you say will stick, meaning that they are not learning.

Here are three ways to open your online (or face-to-face) teaching modules that will grab your students' attention and prepare them to learn.

Why

Faculty think that the mere fact that a topic is part of the class and thus will be on the test should be sufficient to grab students' attention. Well, has experience proven that to be the case? Of course not. The glazed looks in students' eyes during lectures and their cell phone viewing habits prove otherwise. External "motivations" such as grades don't truly motivate us—and often actually undermine performance and learning (see Pink's talk.) We pay attention to what is inherently interesting to us, not to what someone tells us we "have to" pay attention to. Finding that motivating thing is the key to initiating learning.

One way to motivate is to start by telling your students why the topic is important to them. Remember that students are not in school for the grade but rather to prepare themselves for something they plan to do afterward. Connect with that thing.

For instance, I start a medical ethics class for future medical professions with this message:

As a medical professional, you will face situations where you must make ethical decisions, including possibly whether to allow someone to die. You cannot avoid these situations—they will find you—and you cannot avoid having to make a decision that you must defend, maybe even in court. Once in these situations, you will find yourself facing competing and contradictory requests. The patient's son might say, "He told me that he would rather die than be on life support," while the patient's daughter says, "He made it clear in his advance directive that he would want to hold out hope for recovery, and his son was always after his money anyway." In this course, we will talk about how you make and defend those decisions.

Now I have the students' attention because I've expressed the value of the topic in terms of something that is meaningful to them. I have given them a reason to be interested in the topic, and with this foundation, students can start learning.

Question

Another powerful way to get someone's attention is to ask a question. Here is another example drawn from my medical ethics class:

You are the surgeon for a 76-year-old man who needs a kidney transplant. His daughter is the only possible donor, but the pre-op blood work shows that she is not a suitable donor because she is not his biological daughter. Would you tell the man, his wife, or his daughter?

Anyone who sees that question will start formulating answers. One student might say, "I would not say anything to the man or his family because it can only cause hurt without benefit," whereas another might say, "I have to explain why we can't use his daughter, and he has a right to know."

Not only are students psychologically invested in the topic, but the question is also an ideal segue into two important theoretical principles in medical ethics: minimize harm and be honest with patients. Understanding these principles and how they apply to real-life cases is the ultimate purpose of the class, and I have teased the principles out of my students' own responses to the question.

Faculty often start discussing a subject on the theoretical level and then apply the theory to practice. But a more effective practice is to reverse the order by starting with an example that gets students thinking. Now the student has some context in which to understand the theory.

These questions need to be crafted so anyone can answer them on the basis of his or her own intuition and experience. Faculty often make the mistake of asking the class to recall questions about the readings in order to test whether they have done the work. That is testing only their ability to remember information, their confidence that they have it right, and their willingness to look like a brown-noser in front of the other students. No wonder we stand around waiting for someone to answer. Instead, ask students a question that will interest them and that they can answer through their own understanding and views.

Case study

A final way to open a teaching module is with a case study that relates to an important concept that will be covered. One of the classic organizational behavior case studies relates to the *Challenger* explosion. As most people know, a lone engineer at NASA recognized that the O-rings in the shuttle were suffering blow-by on takeoff and that it got worse as the takeoff temperature got lower. The *Challenger* was set to take off on the coldest takeoff day yet, and the engineer tried to stop it. But a committee overruled him, and how they did so illustrates the important principle of groupthink.

A good way to open a module on groupthink is with a video describing that case (an excellent one exists for free). Once you start watching this video, you cannot help but be interested in the characters in the drama and how it plays out. This case study shows students that they will likely encounter groupthink in their future work and demonstrates why it is harmful. The teacher not only has the students' attention but also demonstrates the topic's relevance, and can use this background to begin a more philosophical examination of the concept of groupthink itself.

Whether you are speaking to a face-to-face audience or online, start by grabbing your audience's attention right off the bat. Only then will what you have to say stick with them, allowing real learning to occur.

Reprinted from *Online Classroom,* August 2014.

Develop Online Instructor Presence

by Stephanie Delaney, Seattle Central Community College

What is instructor presence? It's the way that instructors present themselves to the students in the online classroom. It also involves simply being present to students through the regular posting of course materials, discussion posts, and announcements.

Instructor presence increases student retention because students are more likely to stay in class if they feel their instructor cares about them. By being present, the instructor can pull students together, encouraging cooperation and collaboration. Additionally, if things start to go off the rails and a student begins to have problems, an instructor who is present can address those problems immediately.

How does one establish instructor presence in an online class? First, determine your teaching persona. Next, determine which elements to share with the class. Last, create a strategy for regularly expressing those aspects of your persona to your class.

Determine your teaching persona

When thinking about a teaching persona, an instructor might wonder, "How do people describe my teaching?" For answers, go to the audience. Talk to your students. Ask them, "What do you think about my teaching?" Read evaluations from former students, too. Those are always full of information that can help define your teaching style. You might also ask peers who have observed you teaching for their feedback about your teaching persona in face-to-face classes.

People often describe my teaching style as welcoming, as I tend to create a comfortable and open environment for learning. And since that word "welcoming" comes up a lot, it's one of the things that I try to project to my students.

I like to convey to my students that I care about them as people, and that I want their learning to be successful. One way that I convey this is through my late policy. I allow students to submit up to three assignments up to four days late. This allows students ultimate flexibility in when they choose to be late and when they choose to be on time. This policy illustrates that I understand students have busy lives with many things going on, and that sometimes, getting classwork done on time is not the most important item on their to-do list. I explain to students that the reason that I have this policy is because I understand what they're going through in life, I care about them, and I want them to be successful. This, in turn, conveys my teaching persona to my students.

Sharing your teaching persona with an online class

First, I recommend that instructors include a photograph of themselves in the online classroom. It doesn't need to be a personal photograph; in fact, a picture that represents the instructor's teaching persona—any sort of graphical representation of the instructor—would work. In the online classroom, students can't see their instructor, which might create mental distance. And it helps students to have an image in their heads when they're working through the course.

Audio and video are also great ways to communicate your teaching persona. Images, fonts, sharing and contextualizing news from a certain discipline, syllabus policies: all of these are ways to express your teaching persona in the online classroom.

A video is a great way to welcome students into a course. In an asynchronous class, students don't get an opportunity to see the instructor, so a welcome video sets the tone of the class, lets students know what's coming up, and shows students how things will progress through the course. I like to create two welcome videos. I send one out to students two weeks before class begins. In this welcome video I start off with a letter, then finish it up with a little video that just tells the students, "Here's how to log into our online class; here's what some expectations are." Mixing text and video like this allows me to convey a lot of information in a friendly and accessible way.

I send a second welcome video on the first day of class in order to welcome students, introduce them to our online classroom space and the syllabus, and give them all the information they might need to be successful in the course. Through this second welcome video, I talk with my students and express through the inflections in my voice, expressions on my face, and the words I use that I care for them.

Some instructors feel a little hesitant about video. They don't want students to see them, or are uncomfortable with being videotaped. And so they will nix that idea at the beginning, but I encourage instructors to give it a shot just the same. If that trial video works well, perhaps you might consider adding more; the concept would translate easily to brief welcome videos for each course module, rather than just at the beginning of class. Giving students an overview of what's coming up and what to expect in the grand scheme of the class is immensely helpful—and video is a great way to create that context. Other ideas for using audio and video in class are weekly audio updates, which tend to be a lot less stressful than video for some people. Podcasting could be effective as well.

Images and fonts are another way to express your teaching persona. Photos of plants or animals or anything that's relevant to the course would work. A historian might take pictures of historical places near the college, for instance. By posting pictures that are personally important to you, students get a good idea of your teaching persona. When designing an online class, explaining the choices behind particular photos can help students grasp what might otherwise be a very subtle expression of your teaching persona.

Another part of conveying the online persona: fonts. Fonts convey an unspoken style, which I liken to clothing choices, or even handwriting. Although you might automatically use the typical font that comes with a learning management system, you may want to consider a different kind of font that better expresses your personal style.

Yet another way to convey your teaching persona is by sharing current news from the relevant discipline. This helps students understand the enthusiasm you for your discipline and gives them context, as well as conveying up-to-date information about the subject matter of the class. Sharing disciplinary journal articles or discipline-specific features of popular culture articles would work as well, as long as you are deliberate about showing students how the content relates to the course.

Just being cognizant of the daily tasks that a student must go through to be a member of class can show compassion. Discuss textbook options: Can students rent them or do they need to buy books? Provide variety in assignments: allow students to express their own personalities by having various assignments that give them some choice. These can all illustrate perspectives on teaching and make students aware of instructor presence.

I've offered three ways to get started: first, the welcome letter or video. Welcoming students to your class is the absolute best way to begin setting the tone and communicating a teaching persona. Second, course design elements like font, color, and language can make students comfortable in class. Third, communicating discipline-specific news allows students to see the subject matter's relevance and your enthusiasm for it. All of these can lead to a more authentic persona in the online class, with happier and more successful students as the outcome.

Adapted from the Magna 20-Minute Mentor presentation, *How Can I Develop Online Instructor Presence?*

Developing a Course-Specific Orientation

by Rob Kelly

Many institutions offer an orientation to online learning, providing students with a general overview of the learning management system and resources available to help them succeed. It's a nice start, but it doesn't go far enough, argues Anna Stirling, adjunct computer information systems instructor at Mount San Jacinto College and @ONE Online Teaching Certification program coordinator.

Despite an institutional online learner orientation, students in Stirling's online courses were unprepared. Their struggles with the technology often led to missed deadlines, frustration, and sometimes attrition.

The general orientation gave students a good overview of the skills needed to succeed in the online learning environment, "but my students were really struggling with the technology, specifically the technology being used in *my* course," Stirling says.

To address this need for technological support, Stirling embedded just-in-time information throughout her courses. "It was working okay, but I started realizing that they were still struggling with the technology. And sometimes that caused them to lag in completing the coursework," she notes.

She decided to front-load all that technical information into a course-specific orientation, designed to model the design of the actual course. Stirling's orientations provide learners with low-stakes practice activities that they can do repeatedly until they become comfortable with the technology being used in the course.

Like each module in her courses, the course-specific orientation takes approximately nine hours to complete. Orientation activities include reading the syllabus, reviewing course policies and procedures, and completing orientation activities (a check-in, a blog assignment, a student services web search assignment, and a check-in test).

The orientation takes place within the LMS (Blackboard, in Stirling's case) and is available three weeks before the course begins. The official check-in period spans from one week prior to the start of the course until two days after it begins. In order to maintain their enrollment in the course, students must complete at least one activity by the end of the check-in period.

Providing students with access to the orientation before the course begins and requiring them to complete it by the end of the check-in period means that the orientation does not take up valuable course time, a common issue for many online instructors.

In order to proceed to the actual course, students must get a perfect score on the check-in test, which they can take as many times as they need to.

"By having this orientation piece in front and structured similarly to the way the course operates, explaining what students can expect throughout the course, it eliminates that surprise later on in the course, and I think it does it in an engaging way. It's what I consider an active learning experience for the students, rather than just telling them what's in the syllabus. Most instructors do a very good job of explaining textually in the syllabus what's going to be happening later on in the course, but giving students an actual opportunity to interact with the technology in ways that they're going to have to later in the course really reduces that barrier of learning the technology while you're trying to learn the course content," Stirling says.

Also, by modeling the course structure and time commitment, students know up front what to expect in the course "so they can make a determination as to whether they want to stay in the course," Stirling says. "Before, when students didn't have a full understanding of how they were going to use the course, a lot of students would drop three or four weeks into the course. Now, with [the orientation] in the first weeks of the course, students who are not interested in dedicating that amount of time and effort to the course can get out of it relatively quickly and other students can be added. As a result, my retention and success rates have gone up."

Stirling includes the following sections in her course orientations:

1. An introduction

This sets expectations about which tools the course will use, announces the deadline for completing the course orientation, provides a link to the MSJC Online Learner Orientation (an optional general introduction provided by the institution), and lists the learning outcomes of the orientation, which are that students will:

- be able to navigate through the Blackboard course environment for this course,
- know how to communicate using the blog tool,
- know how to upload assignments via the assignment link,
- know how to take a test in Blackboard, and
- know where to find additional help resources.

2. A "before you begin" page

This includes links to the syllabus and schedule, faculty information, a books/resources page, and an introductory video. In the video, Stirling shows the course layout and provides realistic expectations.

3. Course activities

These provide students with opportunities to use LMS tools in a low-stakes setting. Rather than having content-related activities, Stirling has students use the tools to engage in activities that orient them to student support services. This section is the one most likely to vary from course to course. It's where students get a chance to practice using the tools that will be used in the course.

4. Important information

This section lays out the course expectations and breaks down how students should spend their time (for example, three hours per week reading/watching resource materials, three hours per week completing the textbook case problem, and three hours per week completing the activity/discussion blog).

Recommendations for creating a course-specific orientation

1. Don't reinvent the wheel.

Creating course-specific orientations such as those Stirling recommends is a labor-intensive endeavor. This is why she has posted an example of one of her orientations for others to adapt under a Creative Commons license. Here's the URL: *http://bit.ly/DCSOO*.

2. Structure your orientation like the course.

The orientation should follow the same structure as the units in the course: introduction, activities, and assessments. This establishes a familiar course navigation experience.

3. Include activities that provide useful knowledge as well as practice with the tools.

Once you know which tools the course will include, design activities that use each of those tools. Stirling has students engage in activities that introduce them to student support services such as counseling, tutoring, financial aid, and the library. "What are the services that you want your students to know about that will help them be successful?" she asks. "Leverage those with the tools you have and provide any other information you think is important for your students to know before they start your course."

4. Insert your personality into the orientation (and your course).

"I'm a huge proponent of putting yourself into your courses. When you're writing instructions or explanations, write in your own voice. Write your introductions the way you talk so that it puts you and your voice into the course," Stirling says.

Reprinted from *Online Classroom*, August 2014.

How Student Learning Can Begin before the First Day of Class: Establishing Early Connections among Students

by Gary R. Hafer, Lycoming College

The first time my middle school-aged son attended a Major League ballgame, he was astounded by what the players were doing on the field before the game. He saw some of his favorite players contorting in all sorts of positions: balancing, running backwards and sideways, even lying on the ground, some stretching their hamstrings with enormous rubber bands. One player even stood on one leg with outstretched arms. He could not understand why all those moves were required, since he never witnessed a single one of those motions in the game. But even through his misunderstanding, he did recognize something significant: all the players believed in what they were doing, even if he could not see the significance behind their pregame gymnastics. Essentially, my son saw the importance of the practice routine before the big game, even if he did not fully comprehend it. And even more importantly, he witnessed the characteristics of practice the players needed even if they performed in ways not directly related to the practice.

And so it is with college teaching. Students and their professors see the importance of the first day, that big game. But often they do not make the connection with the practice routine, divorced from the look and feel of when they're keeping score during the semester. But even those professors and their students who recognize the primacy of practice can still find it difficult, even impossible, to find enough time on the first day to initiate such practice. After all, there's the syllabus to go over, the structure of the class to introduce, names to learn and mispronounce. There's so many activities for professors to do. And perhaps that's the core problem. It is professors who are explaining, exhibiting, and demonstrating. They are taking on all the activities of practice that they want their students to enact. And while professors are practicing on the field, students assume another role and become the spectators in the stands, wondering why all this practice is necessary before they have to take the field themselves and play the big game.

For us as professors, the pressure to produce a good first-day product mushrooms when we look at what the scholarly literature says about that first day. Worse yet, if we start with a nebulous goal of deep learning, we can find the outcome beyond our reach. For example, we know from some studies that students expect highly structured course material that they can organize in a variety of situations. Without an expansive practice rooted in the first day, the chances for deeper learning in the course are lessened considerably.

Other pedagogical literature documents what activities are the most productive for that first day. Joe Kreizinger, for example, recommends professors establish early connections among students, course matter, and instructor. In one empirical study, Frank LoSchiavo and his colleagues redesigned their introductory social psychology course so that several abstract concepts could be converted into more concrete examples. He had students demonstrate these abstractions in class starting on the first day.

Since students seldom recognize what social psychology entails, the usual rote activities like going over the syllabus waste a lot of precious time that the researchers felt was critical to delivering students to the subject they would be studying.

Similarly, Kim Case and her associates researched students' general expectations for the first day, confirming what reflective teachers generally think about stereotypical opening activities like self-introductions. Specifically, they fail to engage new learners in the class. But perhaps we need go no further than James Lang, who argues persuasively that establishing a class ethos is paramount, and this must start from the premier class.

And the best way I know to establish that ethos is through principal practice: practicing tests, papers, reading and whatever higher-stakes activities we design in our courses. I also know it's impossible to bring all that practice to bear on the first day. Even if professors could, students would soon be overwhelmed, and this is the dissonance we face. We can agree that the first day of class is all-important, but we cannot deliver what is all-important to the first day.

The only way out of this dilemma involves extending that first encounter by reaching out to students using Internet technologies up to one week before the course officially starts. That outreach might be through a letter invitation, an introductory video, an electronic version of the syllabus, a system of direction students can rely on, and/or a head-start homework assignment, all delivered before the first day so we can establish our course dynamic, ensuring the best possible practice on that first day.

This early outreach benefits your course in at least four ways. One: students implicitly see that, through your early communication, the low-level student activity they associate with the first day is dispensed with. Students conclude that something important must be happening on this first day. Two: students relish getting a head start, especially if they are starting college for the first time. By reaching out to them first, instead of them coming to class first, you set a model in motion for the entire semester. Three: practice becomes something integral to the course into which we guide our students. Four: when the semester officially starts, students know what to do so we hit the ground running.

In short, if we can reach out to our incoming students with early communications, we can better match what's promised with and necessary for the first day. When real learning is present on the first day, we can increase the number of practice activities that very first week. For instance, instead of introducing the syllabus on the first day, we could have students read it during Week Zero, the week before classes begin, and start practicing their understanding of it. They're discovering the depth of reading we expect them to fathom in the course. We can do the same with our tests and papers and other persistently underachieving learning events that have disappointed us in our courses, because now we have extended the timeline for practice.

Adapted from the Magna 20-Minute Mentor presentation, *How Can Student Learning Begin before the First Day of Class?*

Set Students up for Success in Online Courses

by Jill Schiefelbein, Impromptu Guru

Student success comes from strong leadership, including establishing rapport, providing resources, and putting the onus of responsibility on the students, rather than the instructor. Perhaps the most important area for success in any online course is what I call the "start here" area. Let's explore this idea further.

"Start here" area

Some instructors call this an introductory area or a "welcome to the course" area. I like calling it "start here," because, quite frankly, it's incredibly descriptive and leaves no room for misinterpretation.

Let's take a look at the six key elements of a start-here area: the instructor introduction video, course expectations, main assignment tutorials, technology tutorials, student engagement areas, and a syllabus quiz.

Instructor introduction

The first thing that an instructor introduction video should do is establish rapport. When students take an online class, one of the most common complaints is that the human touch is lacking. They feel that they don't have an instructor or a professor to interact with, that they're really just interacting with a system. That's why an introduction video is so important: it helps to establish not only the rapport and the human touch, but also a means for students to interpret all future communication, and that cannot be overrated.

Next, an instructor introduction establishes the instructor as a person and a professional, and as the expert on this topic. Also important in the instructor introduction video is the expectation for how students will address the instructor.

And finally, the instructor introduction video should touch on great things about the course or the subject area in general. It's really important from the student perspective to see the instructor's enthusiasm and passion for a topic. When students see that right out of the gate, they are more likely to be engaged and want to be engaged not only with the instructor, but with the course content as a whole throughout the session.

Course expectations

I recommend creating a course expectations video that establishes ground rules and unbreakable policies. This video should also include expectations for student conduct. Establish all important expectations here. If the course includes many interactive elements where peers are interacting with peers, definitely address that in this area.

At this point, it makes sense to touch upon grading expectations as well, or grading philosophy. In my classes, for example, I like to tell students that if you meet the letter of the assignment, meaning that you can read an instruction sheet and follow bullet points, that is average work. That is a "C" grade. If you want "B" grades or "A" grades, you need to go above and beyond.

The last component of a course expectations area involves technical specifications. Here I state, "If you are experiencing technical problems, call tech support," then give students contact information in case of technical difficulties.

Assignment and technology tutorials

Assignment tutorials add different channels to explain a basic text-based instruction sheet, adding audio or video presence to communicate via a different channel, accommodate different types of learners, and reiterate the steps. The other thing these tutorials might explain is the grading and assessment process. This is really important, because students, again, need to know how they're being assessed.

With technology tutorials, I recommend offering one for each new channel of communication that will be used in the course. For students who have never taken an online class before, technology tutorials eliminate confusion and are a means of supporting and supplementing the information that is already out there.

Student engagement

Next, including student engagement in the "start here" area is important. This is not only a means of delivering information, but it's also an opportunity to get students to interact with the instructor, to interact with other students in the course, and to engage themselves with the content before they have even opened the textbook.

The first thing to think about here is that there are three interactivity types: student-to-student interactivity, student-to-content interactivity, and student-to-instructor interactivity. Most of the time in an online course, the student-to-content interactivity is assumed. But student-to-student relationships and student-to-instructor relationships aren't always assumed or nurtured. Establish these within the first week of class.

I recommend a hallway conversation area; some people call this a general discussion forum. This is where students can be social, ask questions, and have the instructor respond or respond to each other, which is really important because students helping students allows them to take responsibility for themselves and each other.

Finally, establish the conversation area as a channel for connection. One of the complaints that a lot of students have in online courses is that they feel disconnected not only from the instructor but from other students. By adding a student engagement element to the start-here or introductory area, students are set up for success from the first day of class.

Syllabus quiz

This area could be called a course introduction quiz, an expectations quiz, or a syllabus quiz. The point of this quiz is to emphasize the important policies that govern the online classroom. Put these in a set of questions that get students to interact with them. In my classes, I like to use an adaptive release here—until students get a perfect 10 out of 10 on this quiz, they cannot proceed into other areas of the course. I love to use the contract question as the last question on the quiz: "True or false, I certify that I have read, understand, and agree to abide by all the terms on the syllabus."

In summary, the six key elements that need to be included in that "start here" area for student success are the instructor introduction, course expectations, main assignment tutorials, technology tutorials, a student engagement area, and the syllabus quiz, that magic quiz that really brings it all home for the students. Plus, if online testing or quizzing will be a part of the course, students get a sample of that right at the beginning of class so there's no ambiguity later.

Adapted from the Magna 20-Minute Mentor presentation, *How Can I Set Students up for Success in Online Courses?*

Online Learning 2.0: Start Your Class with a Video Welcome

by John Orlando, Northcentral University

College faculty focus their job training on learning their subject matter. But subject matter expertise is one of the least important elements that a teacher brings to the table. After all, nearly everything faculty members know about their subjects can be found in some public form somewhere.

Your real value as a teacher is the relationship that you establish with your students. You can look at a student's work, diagnose his or her problems, and provide feedback and advice in a form that the student can understand in order to improve performance.

But accepting this feedback requires a degree of rapport between teacher and student. Adult students in particular want instructors to show their humanity, because they view instructors more as colleagues and co-investigators than as the "sage on the stage."

This is why it is critical to establish a rapport with students right at the beginning of your online courses. The best way to build this rapport is with a video about the class or yourself. A video humanizes you in your students' eyes and opens them to the learning relationship.

Webcam

There are two ways to create a video. One is to simply record yourself speaking to a webcam. This format is best used to discuss the course. You should motivate students by talking about why the course is important, what they will get out of it, and what makes it interesting. This is a chance to connect with students by showing your enthusiasm for the subject matter and for teaching.

The big advantage of webcam recordings is that they are easy to make. Just use your webcam software to record yourself, speaking to the camera as you would to a student sitting in front of you. The disadvantage is that you can't edit the recording without making it jarring for the viewer, as your head moves abruptly from one position to another. This means that you need to use a mistake-free shoot, which will probably require multiple takes. Try not to get frustrated and swat your webcam off your monitor. It won't survive the landing.

Digital biography

The second option is to create a digital biography. Here you will combine audio narration with imagery to take your audience on a journey through your life. This format is ideal for an autobiography because you can include images of the places you have been and the things you have done. The advantages of digital storytelling are that it is much more visually appealing than a webcam recording and that it doesn't require any "acting." It also allows for more creativity, and the result can be edited. The disadvantage is that it is more time-consuming to produce.

In either case, you can post your video to your online classroom if it allows video. If not, put it on YouTube. A YouTube account comes with a Google account, and you can set it to "public" (so that people can reach it with a link) but "unlisted." This also allows students to leave comments if they wish. You will likely find people saying things such as, "I hiked Grey's Peak just last year as well. Amazing views, aren't they?"

Creating a webcam video

Here are some tips for making a webcam video:

- **Speak to the camera, not the monitor.** Many people make the mistake of looking at the monitor while filming, which creates the impression that they are speaking to the viewer's chest, which can make viewers uncomfortable. You're going to have to remember what you want to say and speak to the webcam without notes.
- **It's okay to look away.** Don't try to stare down the webcam. Looking away creates variety and keeps your audience's attention.
- **Be yourself.** It's easy to lose all dramatic expression in front of a camera—to look like a statue and speak in monotone. Try imagining that you're speaking to a live audience. Maybe even tape a photo of an audience just below your webcam. Remember to vary your voice and facial expressions just as you would in front of your class.

Creating a digital biography

Here are some tips for making a digital biography:

- **Use images, not bullet points.** Just as in any presentation, always use images to illustrate your ideas. Bullet points simply distract and confuse the reader. Dramatic images work best.
- **Start by recording the narrative.** The narrative determines pacing, so you always want to record the narrative first in something like Audacity (*http://youtu.be/7_ypzIui2bQ*), and then layer on the images afterward.
- **Focus on your personal, not professional, biography.** I'm sorry to say this, but none of your students care where you went to school or what you published. Did you choose your college classes based on where your professors went to school? I didn't think so. Instead, talk about your personal life and interests. If you do mention your professional work, weave it into a context that would be of interest to your students.
- **Add transitions between images.** Simple transitions such as fade-ins and fade-outs keep your audience's attention.

Start making video introductions to your courses today and see your student engagement increase from the very beginning.

Reprinted from *Online Classroom,* December 2013.

How to Make Online Group Projects More Effective: Establishing Meaningful Relationships in the Online Classroom

by Jean Mandernach, Grand Canyon University

When we look at the value of collaborative group work, the research is clear: group work is beneficial to learning. It improves retention, critical thinking, persistence, motivation, satisfaction, engagement, time on-task, and the list goes on and on. Now, these benefits are not unique to the online classroom. Collaborative group work is valuable whether you're sitting in a face-to-face classroom or in an online classroom. But it's important to remember that some of these benefits are uniquely suited for the online classroom.

Think for a minute about students in an online course. Most of them are sitting at home, maybe at work. They're alone at a computer. It's just them and the monitor. It's not the most engaging atmosphere. Group work gives students the opportunity to enjoy the psychosocial benefits of an online course. It helps them to establish relationships not just with the content and the instructor, but with their peers. It helps them build the skills they need to be successful not only in the online classroom, but in the modern workforce.

So the fact that collaborative group work helps students to be engaged, to spend more time on task, to be more satisfied, and to show more persistence is uniquely valuable in this online classroom. Other, more interesting things than studying are simply a click away; we need to engage students to keep them focused on learning. Online group work provides an opportunity for you to pull students in and engage them in a meaningful way in a social environment that doesn't naturally happen in that online classroom.

The advantages are clear. Students can learn more. They can enjoy more. They're going to build teamwork skills and communication skills. But the reality is there are a lot of practical barriers in the online classroom that make it more challenging to engage in this kind of work.

Students are working asynchronously. They're often adult learners. In many cases, students report to us that they take online classes because they don't have a lot of time. And so when you start to combine these factors—that they're working in a geographically remote area, they are working in an isolated environment—telling students you want them to interact with others can be a challenge.

To address these barriers, there are four important things an instructor needs to do. First, give students a task worth doing. We need to make a truly collaborative activity that requires group interdependence and fosters team-building.

Second, instructors need to get students to *want* to do the work. The research clearly shows that students hate group projects. Now, as I often tell my children, you take medicine because it's good for you. And as I tell my students, you often engage in instructional activities because they're good for you. Not because you enjoy it, but because it's going to teach you important skills that you need to succeed in the workforce. So convincing students that group work is worthwhile for them and that it's worth their time and investment in that group activity becomes important.

Third, teach students how to collaborate in an asynchronous environment. It's natural to do group work when you're all sitting together. It's not as natural when you're each working on your own time, at your own pace, and in your own location. Students need guidance on how that group should interact in a meaningful way.

Last, the instructor needs to have a plan. Group work is not only challenging for students, but it can be challenging for instructors as well. To be effective, instructors need to have a way to manage, grade, and monitor group projects in a meaningful fashion for students (without stressing themselves out in the process).

The best collaborative assignments are authentic. They give students something meaningful to work toward. A collaborative assignment should reflect what students are hoping to do in their careers. Most of us rarely complete activities without any input, guidance, insight, or perspective from the people around us. So think about that—what could a professional do?

Good collaborative assignments can't have a right answer. If there is a single right answer, one student is going to go find that right answer, and they'll complete the project by themselves. And that's not a group project. So think about things in which there are multiple perspectives, in which there's a debate, a controversy, in which different viewpoints could provide different insights to inform that issue or that answer. A research critique would work well.

In this type of assignment, students need clear roles. For instance, an instructor might assign one student as the methodological expert who will think about different ways to investigate the question. His or her job is to think of all the possible methodological concerns and apply them to analyze whether this study did a good job or not. Another student should be in charge of statistics. And someone else can be assigned to going back to the literature. Did the author miss anything? Is there other interesting information that could have informed this research that the author didn't include? What else is relevant that perhaps they failed to mention? Another student is the discussion person. Now you can assign the student groups issues to discuss and debate.

In this way, the assignment becomes a group project. Because it's not feasible for one student to effectively do all those different aspects, instead, all the students come together and apply their own expertise to that critique.

Another good assignment would be to investigate a case study from certain viewpoints. Perhaps one student can look at it from a cognitive perspective, another from a psychological perspective. But each person has a different perspective. Some questions to ask students: What do we know about this? What does the media tell us? What do journal articles tell us? Have any books been written on this? Now, from your perspective, how can we understand this case in a more comprehensive fashion?

Likewise, current event analyses are another project that gets students looking at things from many different angles. Taking on different cultural views in response to a current event could become a good project—students might research a current event in the news in the United States and have one person go out and research it from the German media, while someone else can look at it from the perspective of a South American country or an Asian country, bringing information together in that way. To what extent did the cultural viewpoints and the media twists impact the way we understand this issue?

Notice the key dimension that's shared among all of these projects is that there's no single right answer. And no matter how much students work, there will never be a right answer. There are only informed perspectives and informed opinions that can help students more critically understand the information.

When beginning to plan a group assignment, then, it's important to go beyond just the question of whether or not is it collaborative, although that is essential. You must also begin to question what students need to know in order to do the assignment effectively. Students will need more direction in the online environment than they would in a face-to-face class. When a group of students gets together in the classroom, social cues naturally take over. Students talk and figure out who's a leader and who's a follower, and the natural social environment will give them some guidance and feedback. Online, that natural social environment is lacking, so it is up to the instructor to provide guidance.

In addition, time is a major factor to consider, as things tend to take longer in the online environment. What could be completed in five minutes in a face-to-face classroom might take three or four days by the time one student emails and another student responds, and then another. It's going to draw out the timeline and, thus, the instructor needs to be very clear about deadlines. It's also helpful to inform students of the kinds of roles that will be useful for the project. Giving that kind of overview and guidance on the expectations of the assignment is essential in the online group space.

Once the project is set up, it's time to get students to invest. This is not always easy, as, like the research tells us, students generally care more about the grade than about learning. Whether we like it or not, they repeatedly tell us, what I care about is that end product, because that's what I'm graded on. And when push comes to shove, I'm more concerned about my grade than I am about learning.

So as instructors, giving equal emphasis to the process as well as the product is essential—not only in grading, but also in our approach to students. If they think the final product is the only important part, they have missed out.

Lastly, how does the instructor manage this process? As I mentioned, clarity is key regarding expectations, dates, and the grading process. It is often helpful to establish several check-ins with students throughout the project timeline.

In the end, when it's time to grade, a holistic view on the instructor's part is paramount. Peer review, self-review, and instructor feedback can be combined into a holistic evaluation, not only of *what* was produced, but also the teamwork that went into reaching that final product.

We know group work is valuable. The challenge for online instructors, then, is to structure it in a manner that allows our online students to suc-ceed—and, moreover, to gain the skills and the benefits available from this sort of collaborative social learning that aren't always natural in an online classroom.

Adapted from the Magna 20-Minute Mentor presentation, *How Can I Make Online Group Projects More Effective?*

Three E-learning Design Considerations

by Suzanne Zak, Teachers College, Columbia University

With today's technologically savvy student, the online learning environment should be an effective platform for course delivery. And it is—for some. But attrition rates for online courses remain high. How is it possible to have a nation of higher education students who understand how to operate a plethora of ubiquitous electronic devices, yet they cannot figure out where to go once logged into an e-learning class? What are some of the barriers to e-learning that stand in the way of today's tech-savvy students? How can our online courses be designed to help students navigate and complete them?

Challenges

One of the first challenges for the student in an online environment is understanding the layout of the course. Online learning puts the student in the center or in control of his or her learning (Fee 2009), both in navigating the course and doing the work. Unlike the traditional classroom, where the instructor sets the agenda and determines the content for that class, in an online environment, the student is in control of the experience. The student must be motivated to log on and navigate the environment in order to achieve the desired learning outcomes.

Creating and designing an environment that is user friendly, aesthetically pleasing, and useful seems to be the greatest challenge in promoting student retention and engagement. A study conducted by Robins and Holmes found that, based on appearance, users judge the credibility of a website in 3.42 seconds (Robins and Holmes 2008, 9). In these seconds, students also respond emotionally to what they see. Images can communicate complex concepts in a succinct manner, yet many online environments focus on written content, using words more than imagery. In addition, students can be overwhelmed when they enter an online course for the first time and see too many assignments or areas to navigate.

Announcements page

To help students with their initial login experience, create an announcements page that includes an image or banner on the top and a "read this first" tab on the left-hand side of the page that provides a general overview of the course environment and demonstrates how the course is set up. It is also helpful to include a short video in this section that introduces you and the course layout.

Many LMSs include a calendar or homepage the students are sent to once they log in. If students see another home page when they enter a specific course, they can easily miss assignments that are due. In my teaching experience, having the announcements set as the entrance point for the course helps keep students on task. Most LMSs have the ability to email an announcement, so students can be reminded of upcoming deadlines. Having announcements in both places helps students plan (Ishtaiwa and Abulibdeh 2012).

Consistency is key

With online learning, consistency from the educator and course environment seems to be key in keeping students engaged throughout the semester. Besides the discussion board, emails are the number one source of communication. Online learning environments are largely asynchronous by nature. The advantage to online learning is its flexibility, allowing students to access course information and complete assignments 24/7. While the educator is not expected to be "on" 24/7, timely responses to students' questions, problems, or concerns can help maintain forward momentum. In a regular semester, it is not unreasonable for students to expect a response from their instructor within 24 to 36 hours during weekdays. The more consistent and timely the communication, the better the rapport that develops between the students and teacher, helping students feel connected to the class and content.

Consistency with course content and deadlines is essential for student success. An online course environment typically employs weekly or biweekly lessons. Educators who faithfully stick to their schedules create a consistency for students to follow, enabling predictability that can help students keep on task. Students become accustomed to an online rhythm that usually entails reading, watching a video, listening, or writing. It is of utmost importance to keep those tasks consistent throughout the semester.

Three elements of course design that make a big difference in course completion for students include a course layout that is aesthetically pleasing and uses pictures and text, not text alone; communication from the educator; and consistent schedules and activities. Keeping these elements in mind will greatly add to the success of your online course!

References

Fee, K. *Delivering E-Learning: A Complete Strategy for Design, Application, and Assessment* (1st ed.). London: Kogan Page, 2009.

Ishtaiwa, F. F., and E. S. Abulibdeh. "The Impact of Asynchronous e-Learning Tools on Interaction and Learning in a Blended Course. *International Journal of Instructional Media* 39 no. 2 (2012): 141–159.

Robins, D., and J. Holmes. "Aesthetics and Credibility in Web Site Design." *Information Processing & Management* 44 no. 1 (2008): 386–399. doi:10.1016/j.ipm.2007.02.003

Reprinted from *Online Classroom*, July 2014.

CHAPTER 2

•

Building Rapport with Students

Online Learning 2.0: It's Time to Create Real Faculty Bios

by John Orlando, Northcentral University

In an age where a school's webpage is its most important informational tool, most websites now include faculty biographies. But what do you find in those bios? The faculty member's PhD-granting institution, publications, research interests, etc. In other words, nothing that is of any interest to a student. Nobody cares where a faculty member got his or her PhD. Did you pick your undergraduate courses based on where the professors received their PhDs? Of course not.

For some reason, school websites are designed on a "show them the factory" mentality. It is akin to going to Amazon's website to purchase a computer and being given pictures of the company's warehouses. Faculty bio pages are not for projecting a CV. They are for communicating with students. This is especially true when the bio is inside an online classroom.

Faculty need to create bios that speak to students by providing information that is relevant to them. Here are some types of content that could go into a relevant and engaging faculty bio.

Teaching philosophy

What does a student most want to know when browsing for a course? Obviously, what it will be like to actually take the course. That means that a great way to start a faculty bio is by describing your teaching philosophy. Do you spend class time lecturing or in discussion with students? Are you flipping the class by putting most of the content online and devoting face-to-face time to discussion or other student activities? Will students be expected to participate in every class, perhaps as a part of their grade? The bio is an opportunity to talk about your teaching style and how that plays out in the structure and expectations of the course.

The bio is also an opportunity to talk about how you will assess students. In order to succeed, students need to understand how they will be assessed and what standards of excellence they will be expected to achieve. Is the class primarily focused on improving a student's writing skills and thus heavily essay-oriented, with writing quality being the primary assessment criterion? Is the class focused on teaching technical knowledge, as demonstrated by weekly assignments that require students to solve problems? These are the sorts of questions that are relevant to students' course decisions. The information may weed out students who would not do well in your type of course and will better prepare students who do come in, thus producing better work.

Personal bio

The faculty bio is also a good opportunity to start laying the groundwork of the learning relationship by humanizing yourself. There is no law requiring faculty to focus on their professional achievements. Personal achievements are more important to building a relationship, and much more memorable. How many students tell their friends that "My engineering prof went to Cornell" rather than "My engineering prof spent three years studying Buddhism in Tibet"?

Anything that makes you interesting is good fodder for a bio. The best faculty photo I've ever seen online showed the faculty member in a scuba suit with bags of golf balls in each hand. He explained that he dredges the local golf course pond for balls every spring. Notice how I remember that fact? How many faculty photos do you remember? A good rule of thumb when writing a bio is that we are interested in things that are interesting, not in things that are not interesting.

Now, you could include information about your professional life if it is tied to something of interest, such as your teaching style or beliefs. For instance, I tell people that I was a business major in college until I spent a year studying in Rome, which transformed my whole outlook on life and turned me into a philosophy major. I then discuss my outlook and how it is reflected in my teaching.

This melding of the personal and professional also provides an opportunity to talk about why you find your subject interesting. Contagious enthusiasm is a powerful motivator, and we learn much better when we are given the significance of the subject matter. A civil engineering professor might talk about how he or she was drawn into the profession by the challenge of developing structures that are both functional and beautiful. He or she might say that many of our greatest cultural monuments, such as the Hoover Dam and the pyramids, are a result of civil engineering and that civil engineers get to work on things that will outlive them.

Also consider adding a video to your bio. (See "Start Your Class with a Video Welcome" in Chapter 1.) Posting a video bio might encourage your students to do the same.

So start using your faculty bio to really communicate with students, and find out how it makes a difference to your students and in your teaching.

Reprinted from *Online Classroom*, March 2014.

Using Social Media to Provide Student Support

by Rob Kelly

In spring 2012, Angela Starrett, a mathematics instructor at the University of South Carolina Upstate, was teaching calculus, business calculus, and several other higher-level math courses. To provide students with extra support, she invited them to text her when they had questions. They took her up on the offer, sending images of problems they were struggling with, and she responded in a timely manner. This support seemed to motivate her students. They kept working on problems when they received quick responses from her. However, she found that the students often asked the same questions. Her solution was to use social media, initially Twitter and later Facebook and several other tools, to move this basic idea of one-to-one support to one-to-many and, ultimately, many-to-many.

"I thought Twitter seemed like a great idea because it's like the text message environment, but it provides a way for everybody to see what's being discussed," Starrett says.

In addition to her upper-level courses, she implemented social media in her general education college algebra course, which, as at most institutions, had notoriously high failure and withdrawal rates.

Since incorporating social media into her college algebra courses, Starrett has seen a dramatic reduction in student failure and dropout rates. Normally 40 to 44 percent of students in this course would get a D or F, or would withdraw. Now, just 9 percent of students in the course receive a D or F or withdraw from the course.

24/7 support

"Students loved it. They loved that illusion of my 24/7 availability. They also loved not having to go into Blackboard. They loved not having to email me, since so many students don't do email," Starrett says.

One of the advantages of using social media is that students who may be reluctant to seek help themselves can access the help provided to other students. It has also led to "organic collaboration," where students help each other. In some instances, students will simply direct their classmates to resources that Starrett has provided. But in other cases, knowledgeable students will actually help other students.

Students are more likely to offer help on Facebook, where they can join a private group especially for the course, whereas students don't necessarily follow each other on Twitter.

Starrett does not require her students to participate in the social media elements of her courses and offers no incentives, but they see the value of it and do participate. She attributes the widespread participation to the younger generation's familiarity with social media, the ubiquity of mobile devices, and the ability to operate outside the LMS.

"I have asked students why they answered a question [from a classmate]. Usually the response is something like, 'I was sitting there watching a movie, and it came up as a notification on my phone and I thought I'd answer it. I knew the answer,'" Starrett says. "These kids have grown up in an environment where there's a face-to-face personality and an online personality. The online personality is confident, bolder, and helpful, and likes to make comments."

Another important factor in students' willingness to participate is feeling comfortable asking questions. To avoid embarrassment, students have the option of asking questions without being identified to their classmates (though Starrett knows who's asking). "Students know that they can be safe asking a question. Nobody is going to embarrass them because they're asking a question, and the learning is actually becoming a community event instead of happening in isolation. That is the ideal that we hope for in learning environments," says Lori Tanner, former director of a quality enhancement plan called Student Technology Enrichment Program—Upstate and current director of education workforce training in Cyberinfrastructure Technology Integration at Clemson University.

This immediate help contributes to students' willingness to continue their efforts. "There's so much research that points to the millennial and neo-millennial need for instant gratification. When teaching this generation, if you don't answer their question, they will close their book or computer and say, 'Oh well. I tried.' Social media gives them the ability to ask the question right when it comes up, get an answer, and keep moving forward," Starrett says.

Tanner adds, "Some of the feedback we got from students was, 'I knew I would never be lost, because I could get an answer in the middle of the night. It might not be my instructor; it might be a student who had the same problem.'"

Students must be clear about the problems they're experiencing in order to get help. "I really harp on the students about communicating the question. Especially in a math class, so often you get students who say, 'I don't get it. I don't understand.' I won't answer in social media until they tell me what they don't understand, even if it's, 'I have no clue how to start this problem,'" Starrett says.

Different students require different types of support. "For most students, I will correct their wrong step so they can finish the problem. Or I will do a similar work problem. As I get to know how the students learn, I adjust that. I have a few students who have certain disabilities with math, so I know I am going to have to help them out with a few more steps and more explanation," Starrett says.

Tweeting images or sending them via Facebook is a common way for students to ask for help. With Inkflow Plus (*qrayon.com/home/inkflow/*), an iPad app, Starrett can use a stylus to write on the image that a student has sent. For more detailed explanations, she uses the iPad app Doceri (*doceri. com/*).

The design of her course and the use of social media have enabled Starrett to teach a relatively large number of students. In the fall, she will teach 450 students.

Video lectures

Rather than lecturing in a face-to-face class, Starrett records her PowerPoint-based lectures in Camtasia (*techsmith.com/camtasia.html*) and posts them on YouTube. The only homework that students have is to watch the videos and take notes. Starrett breaks them into five- to eight-minute sections. The decision to replace live lectures with video came after Starrett tried using a Twitter backchannel in her lectures.

"I found the [live] lectures to be a complete and utter waste of time, because students do not have a 50-minute attention span no matter how many bells and whistles you add," Starrett says. "Students tell me they watch my videos two or three times until they get it. Between the social media and the way I've flipped the environment, I see motivation and confidence just grow throughout the semester. It's really amazing for students who had a hard time passing algebra in high school."

Each week, students attend the algebra lab for 150 to 250 minutes.

There they work on problems on their own device or a zero client machine in the lab. Once they master the learning objectives, they take a quiz.

Online version

Starrett mostly teaches using this flipped approach, but she has also taught college algebra totally online. Based on students' preferences, the course used Facebook to provide social media support. Facebook also was the forum for the dialogue that would typically take place in the face-to-face math lab.

As in the face-to-face version of the course, the social media support in the online version took place outside the LMS, which improves students' ability to access it wherever they might be using a mobile device, without having to log in to the course.

Advice

Starrett sees the potential of social media use in a variety of disciplines. "I definitely think [it is helpful in] any subject that lends itself to being more visual, where the explanation of something tends to be a picture," she says.

She offers the following advice on getting started:

- **Dip your toe in the water.** If you want to incorporate social media into your course, begin with a platform that you have some familiarity with, one where you already have a personal account. If you don't have a personal account, set one up. "Get used to how the system works. Follow some colleagues, peers, or friends. Just get comfortable with the mechanism of the social media, and give yourself a summer or semester to try to implement that in your course.

- **Market the concept to students.** "I think sometimes students' motivation is linked to how you sell it to them. I market it as 24/7 availability, fulfilling that need for instant gratification—not as a mandate, not as an assignment," Starrett says.

Reprinted from *Online Classroom*, March 2014.

Building Online Learning Communities

by Rob Kelly

Whenever Barbara Polnick teaches online, she pays special attention to fostering a community of learners, focusing both on the design of the course and the way she facilitates it.

Polnick, an associate professor in the educational leadership program at Sam Houston State University, bases her approach to online learning communities on the following four components of a learning community:

- **Spirit**—This refers to students' sense of belonging, which often builds over time as a matter of course, particularly among learners who go through a program as a cohort. In an online course that is not cohort-based, the instructor needs to be deliberate in fostering this sense of belonging.
- **Trust**—Trust builds on spirit. "If you have a sense of belonging and acceptance, a belief that people are going to value your opinions, it leads to feeling safe speaking out openly," Polnick says. "It's the feeling of being supported—not necessarily agreed with, but supported and able to express your opinions.
- **Interaction**—This refers to a "sense that working together helps you accomplish your own personal goals. It isn't just about feeling good; it's also about the notion that these people contribute to you being more successful, that sense of believing that interaction helps you achieve your goals," Polnick says.
- **Learning**—This is the notion of working together to achieve a common goal—co-constructing meaning to better understand the course content and feeling that other learners have helped clarify ideas for you.

Make connections

Creating a learning community takes time. It helps to begin as early as possible, preferably before the course even begins. Once she knows who will be in her online course, Polnick asks students to fill out information profiles. In the case of this program, for example, it's useful to know where the students work, whether it's in a school or business, as well as their leadership experience.

She makes it point to acknowledge that she has read their profiles and tries to make connections based on the information so that the profile creation doesn't just seem like an assignment. "I'll say things such as, 'You teach math. I used to teach math.' Or, 'You have two kids. So do I,'" Polnick says.

Throughout the course, Polnick asks students to share information about themselves that relates to the content. For example, in a leadership course, she asks students to "share with the class three attributes that you think contributes to you being a good leader." The second part of that prompt involves finding three other people in the course who have similar characteristics, which helps create connections among the students.

Polnick also encourages her students to share personal information with each other and to include a photo, so that every time they post in the LMS, that picture appears. "This helps students identify and remember each other." (E.g., "He's the one who's teaching in a rural classroom and has cows.")

It's not enough to have students respond to discussion prompts and to classmates. Polnick also requires that students relate the discussion to their own work situations. "I ask them to make connections wherever possible," she says.

Polnick uses students' personal information, interests, and characteristics to form small groups. For example, she may ask students to rate their technological skills. Depending on the goals of the assignment, she may form homogeneous or heterogeneous groups. To further bond these groups, she has students discuss group norms.

Establish relevance of the learning community

Throughout her online courses, Polnick connects the notion of the learning community to the course content. For example, she'll explain, "As leaders, you will need to work with different kinds of people."

In addition, Polnick recommends pointing out the contributions of others in the feedback one provides, particularly in threaded discussions. "I try to make sure I emphasize not just their response to a question but their interactions with other students. I might say, 'In interacting with Jose and

Martha, you provided specific example of how you use this in the classroom. That was very beneficial to the group,'" Polnick says. "It's a way of letting them know that what they're doing is very important."

Forced dependency

Another way to foster a learning community is to create situations that foster interdependence among group members. This can include limiting resources so that only one person in the group has access to materials and has to share with the group, causing the group to find ways to work within this constraint and to bond while doing so.

Technical support

Technical support is important in all online courses, but it is particularly important if you are trying to foster a strong online learning community. Students need to have reliable access to the course when they are dependent on each other.

Recruit scouts

Monitoring the student experience is an important part of maintaining a learning community. Polnick does this with the help of scouts—the two or three most conscientious students in the course. "I can tell from the first two weeks of class who is always going to be ahead. They're usually the first people to post their student information profiles. They're the first people who take the syllabus quiz," Polnick says.

She asks these students to go through the course and alert her to things such as broken links and unclear instructions. She also asks them to provide feedback on course activities.

Assessing the learning community

Feedback from scouts and observing the interaction in the course can give you a sense of the strength of a learning community. Other indicators are the quality of work that students produce and the way they relate to the content and each other.

Discussion boards are good indicators of the strength of the learning community. When a learning community is thriving, students indicate they recognize that diversity of opinion is important and note how other students' ideas connect with their own. "If I read that in their work—and that's one of my expectations—then I know they're learning. My main goal isn't that they be a community of learners. My main goals are that they're learning and that they're meeting the learning objectives. So I'm looking at the end result. If the end result is that they're learning and I'm using these strategies to get there, I figure the strategies are working," Polnick says.

In addition to assessing students' learning, Polnick conducts a 20-question survey at the end of each course to assess the learning community, asking, among other things, the extent to which students believe that their ability to perform well in class was built on their own abilities and the additional benefit of working with others. "It helps me plan the next semester," says Polnick.

"A lot of times it's so subtle. Students may not even be aware that it is a learning community. They may focus more on what they're learning and just know that they're comfortable," she says.

Reprinted from *Online Classroom*, April 2014.

From Barely There to Fully Present: Three Ways to Improve Your Instructor Presence

by Diane Monsivais, the University of Texas at El Paso

I recently received a frantic phone call from a distraught colleague who had just received her student evaluations after teaching her first online course. Tearfully, she shared with me sample student comments such as, "I didn't get any feedback on my assignments until it was too late to help me with the next assignment," and "I never heard from my instructor. It was like she was barely there."

Frustrated because she felt that she had been doing a good job of communicating with her students, and also fearful because her adjunct position depended in part on receiving positive student evaluations, she asked for help in setting up an improvement plan for the next course.

Unfortunately, my colleague's frustrating experience is not uncommon for instructors new to the online environment. Managing instructor presence—students' perceptions of how instructors interact with them and guide their learning during a course—is the key to overcoming that frustration. It's not unusual for instructors and students to have widely different perceptions of instructor presence during the same course.

For instructors who may be teaching multiple courses and spending large blocks of time answering student email, the time spent on their courses makes them feel fully present and fully engaged. To students, however, who may be looking for interaction from the instructor on the course discussion boards, it may seem the instructor is "barely there" because there is little trace of him or her in the course.

How would your students rate your instructor presence on a continuum from "barely there" to "fully present"? If there's a difference between your *students'* perception and *your* perception of your instructor presence, you can improve your presence with some simple strategies.

After working with online students at all levels of higher education for more than a decade, I've developed a three-step approach for creating a strong instructor presence. In this article, I describe those steps, giving you a clear plan that can save time, improve the learning environment, and result in positive student evaluations.

Step 1: Interact early and share your plan with the class

About a week before the course starts, send a welcome note reminding students the course will be starting. Include information they might need immediately, such as how to access the course and recapping key information, such as reminding them about the book being used.

At the beginning of the course, be transparent about your interaction plan. Planned interactions range from daily attention to questions, guidance, and problems to weekly formal feedback on assignments. Normally, the most pressing questions students have are when their questions will be answered and how soon the assignments will be graded, so addressing those up front decreases anxiety. Here's an example:

I will normally be checking into the course twice a day, so if one of your classmates doesn't answer, I will do so within a fairly short time. You will receive feedback on postings and assignments in time to use it for any needed improvements on future work.

Your daily and weekly times for course interaction should be on your work calendar, just as showing up for a traditional face-to-face class would.

Step 2: Check in daily and interact if needed

Check in often to the course discussion board that is set up for questions, monitor your course email, and post any announcements as needed. How often is often enough will depend on the length and level of the course. For graduate students in a seven-week course, I check at least twice a day. When students find they are getting prompt responses to questions, their anxiety levels decrease. This short check-in routine becomes a time-saver because students don't send individual emails or create chaos by giving each other incorrect information. Even if it's a five-minute check-in first thing in the morning and/or late at night, it should be a planned routine that is part of your work flow.

Be clear about the days you may not check in as often, whether that is on weekends or certain weekdays. Travel days may also be times when you cannot respond within your usual timeframe. Because most of our students are employed full-time during the week, weekends are when many of them focus on their classwork. For those students, instructor availability on Saturdays and Sundays is critical.

Some specifics about the discussion board

Directions for the discussion board should tell students to post any questions related to the course on the discussion board rather than sending the instructor individual emails. Some students resist making their questions public, so an encouraging note on the discussion board itself saying, "Other students will be grateful you asked" is a way to encourage those who may be reluctant to ask. Here is an example:

Please post all course-related questions or concerns on the discussion board set up for that purpose. Both students and faculty are expected to contribute to replies. Even if you find yourself a little hesitant to ask questions in a public area (for fear that everyone in the world knows something you don't!), just go ahead and ask. I can guarantee if you have a question about something, there are at least five of your classmates wondering the same thing, and they will be overwhelmingly grateful to you for asking. How do I know this with such great certainty? Because it happens every semester, over and over! Some of our most interesting discussions sometimes happen on this discussion board, so please just jump in. (Reserve email for those events that pertain to you personally.)

Some specifics about email

Reply to any individual emails about course content by thanking the student for the question and letting that student know that since others will benefit from the response, he or she should post the question on the course questions discussion board and that you will answer it there. The only emails from students should be related to individual personal issues such as problems that interfere with coursework. Here's a sample response to an email asking a course-related question:

Thanks for asking this question. I think your classmates may also be wondering about that and would benefit from clarification. Please post your question on the course discussion board; I will respond there.

Some specifics about announcements

Post announcements at least weekly. The announcement board is a great place to provide the following information:

- **General assignment feedback**—Give group feedback about an assignment, or use exemplars of student work to model an "A" assignment.
- **Clarification about a general issue**—If a few students have been asking the same type of question on the discussion board or it's clear there is confusion about anything in the course, the announcement area is a great place to reach everyone.
- **Encouragement**—Provide calm reassurance about problems that may be beyond the students' control, such as university tech issues.

Step 3: Grade and summarize (at least) weekly

Set aside specific times each week for grading and posting summaries/synthesis for the week. This can be a time-intensive task, depending on the number of students and the particular assignment. It's better to set aside more time than you may need at first. I generally block the morning after an assignment is due to grade and provide feedback.

Students' ability to improve their next posting may be based on the feedback you provide, so if the next posting is due before you provide that feedback, they miss the chance to use your feedback for improvement. Students should receive feedback on weekly assignments within 48 hours so they can incorporate suggestions for improvement into the next assignment. The interaction plan is your pledge to your students, so make sure to honor the response times you have promised.

End-of-the-week discussion board summaries are an effective way to highlight points you think are important, demonstrate synthesis of ideas, and perhaps clarify misunderstandings that have arisen.

Summary

With student satisfaction and your teaching career at stake, a strong instructor presence can produce big payoffs. By applying these practical strategies, you'll be amazed at how quickly your "barely there" presence rating will move to "fully present," resulting in an improved learning environment and positive student evaluations.

Reprinted from *Online Classroom*, July 2014.

Fostering Personal Connections for a Better Online Learning Environment

by Rob Kelly

Before her online courses begin, Susanne Chuku, assistant professor of economics at Westfield State University, sends each of her students a personal welcome email. "I like to write their names so they know that I took the time to email them personally rather than send a single email addressed to all of them," she says. It sets a welcoming tone and enables students to feel comfortable enough to share additional information about themselves, often including their struggles with the subject matter—typically half of Chuku's students respond with messages of their own. "This is my first step in getting to know them," she relates. "It's the first opportunity they have to talk to me, and I feel it lowers the barrier between the instructor and the students."

The welcome email is part of a strategy to get students to share with her, and ultimately with each other, and to create a more engaging and successful learning environment. Throughout the course, Chuku takes note of the information that her students share in order to strengthen the relationship and make the learning relevant.

Discussion feedback

Chuku generally does not participate in weekly discussions, but she does provide feedback at the end of the week, explaining why each student received the number of points they did. "I relate my feedback to what I know about them. [...] I let them know I understand where they're coming from and maybe even find similarities between the student and me because whenever you have similarities with another person you feel more connected," Chuku says.

To that end, Chuku maintains an Excel spreadsheet to have a handy source of information about her students. She refers to the spreadsheet whenever she provides feedback (particularly in the beginning when she is still learning about her students). This approach is manageable in Chuku's courses—her Principles of Macroeconomics and Principles of Microeconomics courses typically have 20 to 25 students each.

During the first two weeks of discussion, students typically do not engage in very meaningful ways because they have yet to develop trust. They often state that they agree with each other and typically don't share personal information. After a while, they get more comfortable with each other and with relating the content to their lives.

To help facilitate these meaningful exchanges, in her weekly feedback to individual students, Chuku encourages students to disagree with each other, reminding them to be respectful and professional.

Chuku is careful to not be too harsh in her discussion board grading and feedback so she doesn't discourage participation. "Obviously, students cannot write complete nonsense, but the discussions are, for me, more of an encouragement to get students to talk to each other," she says.

In addition, Chuku views the discussion board as a means of understanding her students' perspectives and a way to gain insights into how well they understand the content without the fear of losing a significant number of points. "If I grade them harshly, I believe they will hold back and not be as open as they otherwise would be," she says.

Check in

After each exam, Chuku calculates each student's overall grade and provides individual feedback and encouragement via email. "That particular email has really made a difference because students now ask, 'What can I do to improve my score?' or say, 'Thank you. I have done this because you recommended it, and I'm doing better now.' This really has led to better student outcomes," she says.

In her larger classes, Chuku typically writes two or three sentences in each of these check-in emails and often provides more detailed feedback in smaller classes. "I want students to know it's personalized feedback, not just feedback that I copy and paste to everyone," she says. "I check my Excel spreadsheet and try to make connections. It sounds like a lot of work, but once you get used to it, I think it's doable."

Reprinted from *Online Classroom*, November 2014.

Improving Student Motivation with Check-Ins

by Alisha Etheredge, Strayer University

Students naturally start losing motivation in a college course over time. This is an even bigger problem in online courses, where students can easily feel distanced from the instructor and each other. As an instructor, I notice this as a steadily deteriorating quality of student work during the course. But I found that scheduling a check-in near the beginning of the course often reverses the trend.

I like to do the check-in soon after the course starts, within the first three weeks. This is to show students that I care and to nip any early problems in the bud. The check-in also helps establish a relationship with the student. From this baseline, I can then follow up with more messages throughout the course, returning to issues that came up in the first check-in.

I divide my students into two groups for my check-in: those with a course average above 80 percent, and those below 80 percent. For those above 80 percent, I send out a simple email that recognizes their work:

Congratulations on a successful start to our course! I didn't want your hard work to go unnoticed. You're doing a great job keeping up with the assignments and actively participating in the discussions. Please do not hesitate to let me know if you have any questions or concerns. Remember, I am here to help you throughout our short five weeks together.

I will also add observations on things that each student is doing particularly well and anything that he or she could still work on. Again, the point is to demonstrate that I am tracking their performance as individuals and that I am here to help.

For the students below 80 percent, I look at what is bringing their grade down. Are they missing an assignment? Is the quality of their work below par? Are they not following assignment instructions? I then send out a very simple email to those students that might have the following start:

Subject: Is Everything Okay?

I just wanted to reach out because I noticed that you did not get off to a great start in our course. Although you submitted all your assignments, your performance on them was not as high as it could have been. Please reach out to me if I can be of any assistance. Review my feedback to you on your assignments, and contact me if you have any questions on it. I want you to do well in the course, and I know that you are able to do it. Hang in there!

After sending the message, I find that many students open up and let me into their world. They explain why they are not performing well or why they were not able to turn an assignment in. The information that they provide allows me to more effectively personalize my future communications with them. Instead of saying, "Why aren't you performing well on your work?" I can say, "I know it's tough taking care of a five-month-old, working full time, and going to school, but I know you can do it. Here are some tips for sneaking in some study time at different points throughout the day."

Students are always very appreciative and let me know that it meant a lot to receive that type of recognition. Here is one such response from a student:

Wow! Thank you!! That means a lot. You are the first instructor to send something like this. I appreciate the positive encouragement.

I have learned that the simple act of demonstrating your concern for students goes a long way. It can be easy for instructors to become cynical about student effort and fall into a "time clock" mentality of just going through the course motions. Students pick up on this and react accordingly. A simple check-in will make a world of difference in student performance. Since starting this practice, I find my students are more engaged in the course—posting in the discussions earlier, responding to more of their classmates' posts, and putting more effort into their weekly assignments. And to think … it all starts with a simple email.

Reprinted from *Online Classroom*, October 2014.

How to Keep from Going MIA in Your Online Course

by Steve Dwinnells, Eastern Kentucky University

As an adjunct professor and one who works daily with faculty in helping them understand online education, I have noticed and heard of increasing numbers of professors going missing in action (MIA) while teaching their online course. This is particularly disturbing because engagement is the number one characteristic that faculty must strive for when teaching from a distance.

Being MIA can take several forms. There is the extreme of providing no communication, feedback, or encouragement to students. In this case, the online course becomes nothing more than a self-directed correspondence course. Another form is when feedback is either not constructive or it arrives too late for the student to improve in subsequent assignments. Yet another form of going MIA is lack of presence in interactive assignments such as blogs or discussion boards. So what can we do to prevent going MIA?

- **Set times to "go to class."** I always recommend that my students imagine their online course as a face-to-face course and "attend" on a regular basis two or three times a week. The same holds true for the professor. By "going to class," you can catch up on grading assignments, respond to emails, and provide meaningful guidance that helps keep your students on task. This will also prevent you from falling behind and becoming discouraged yourself.
- **Find ways to personalize your course with your presence**. Include media such as a welcome video at the beginning of the course, or insert media at the start of each module so that the students can see or hear you, and consider using video/audio feedback for some assignments. In addition, occasionally include a video or audio segment within your announcement section so your students can once again

make a connection with more than a computer. How does this help you to not go MIA? When you personalize your course, the students will sense your presence repeatedly throughout it, and you will feel more invested in the course and more likely to remain engaged.

- **Seek opportunities to engage students in creative ways.** As with any discipline, teaching online is not something one learns overnight. One professor I know writes personalized emails to two or three students a week with nothing more than a positive affirmation of some task the student performed that week. Another professor responds to writing assignments using a self-recorded Adobe Connect session so that the student can see and hear the critique. He finds this produces responses even more quickly than typing out or marking up a written assignment. Use a product such as VoiceThread to respond to discussion board postings—again, this is another way to help students feel you are present by virtue of seeing and hearing you.

- **Use discussion boards wisely and often.** Despite the calls for instructor-free student discussions, it is wise to intervene regularly, for several reasons. First, just as in a face-to-face course, you can prevent the session from going off topic. Students can quickly veer off point, but your presence helps keep them focused and on task. Second, students will know that you care about what they are saying. They know you will be looking at their responses—responses that can be praised, critiqued, or called upon for more critical thinking. And finally, by remaining active in a discussion board, you can monitor any inappropriate responses. Your presence will certainly alleviate the fear that you have somehow gone MIA.

- **Remember that online does not mean off-line.** Just because the content, assignments, and assessments are online does not mean that the actual teaching and instructor presence can be off-line. One could have a beautifully designed online course, but with an off-line professor, the learning experience will lack the depth, breadth, and richness of a true learning experience. You may not see your students, but that does not mean they do not see you or are not looking for you. Make yourself available through virtual office hours. Once a week, open up a synchronous session using Adobe Connect or a chat function during which students may come to talk with you. Better yet, conduct a review session prior to a quiz or exam. Remember that teaching online is not a spectator activity—it is a participative one!

Reprinted from *Online Classroom*, February 2016.

Scaffolding Learning

by John Orlando, Northcentral University

I recently took a canoe paddle-making course with my son from an instructor who guaranteed that all participants would come away with a result that they could be proud of. One of the ways he ensured this was by giving us various "scaffolds" at different points in the process that helped us channel our work in the proper direction. Instead of starting with unformed wood, we were given pieces that already had the broad cuts made in them. This allowed us to concentrate on the detailing that forms the real heart of paddle-making. At each step we were provided with the proper tools needed to complete the job and clear instructions on how to do so. As advertised, we all walked away with a result we were proud of and a deep understanding of the paddle-making process.

Good teaching often involves scaffolding learning. Unfortunately, teachers often forget this. As an undergraduate, I was generally given assignments with no more direction than to write a paper of X length on Y topic. This leads many students to head off in entirely the wrong direction from the get-go. Failing miserably like this does nothing to teach and only produces discouragement. Faculty sometimes think that scaffolding is "doing the assignment for the student," but it is not. It is providing the student with the tools needed to succeed.

Scaffolding comes in two forms. Conceptual scaffolds provide the learner with help knowing "what to consider," such as what to look for in a reading (Hannafin, Land, and Oliver 1999), whereas strategic scaffolds help learners complete specific tasks, such as writing a paper. Let's take a closer look at each.

Conceptual scaffolds

Students often do not know what they should be getting out of a reading. Faculty can help direct students to the correct content by providing a list of questions that students should consider as they do their readings. For instance, the questions can track the argument turns in the work so that students are able to follow the writer's thinking, as well as learning that the argument structure is what they should be reading for. The scaffolding also helps students learn how to take notes on their own.

While the questions can be added to the assignment directions, students often forget those questions once they get into the weeds of the reading. A more effective method is to provide some sort of response system that requires students to answer the questions during or after the reading.

One technique I use is to provide assignments as PDFs with fillable forms. I include not only the directions, but also questions for students to answer right on the form while doing the reading. A PDF works better than a Word document because entering information into a Word document shifts the rest of the text. To make a fillable PDF, write out the assignment as a Word document and draw in text boxes after each question. Then convert the document to a PDF using Adobe Acrobat or another PDF conversion tool. Make sure to indicate that you are saving it as a PDF with "text-enabled fields" and the system will convert the boxes to fillable forms.

The questions need not be graded, though students can be told that they will lose points for not answering them. The goal is simply to get students thinking during their reading, which will help with student understanding and knowledge retention. Plus, the instructor can use the responses to identify where students might be struggling and need additional help.

Faculty can also provide some general context and information about the argument in a work as a head start to the student's reading. Many instructors expect students to do a reading before class and come prepared to discuss it. But in a sense this is backwards, because students will get more out of a reading if they are first given some information about it that will help them understand it. Faculty should first discuss the arguments in a reading during class, then provide students with questions that they can answer while doing the reading to help them know what to get out of it. Using this process, students have a scaffold that will ensure that they understand the material and learn what the instructor intended them to.

Online faculty can also scaffold student understanding of course content. I use short videos to deliver content that I create for my online course. I scaffold student viewing of my videos by putting the videos into Google Forms, with each video followed by a question that the student must answer. Student answers get compiled into a spreadsheet that is automatically created in Drive. Then I can view the answers for each student or the entire class at once. This ensures that students watch the videos and engage with the material and also alerts me to common problems that they might be having with the concepts. As teachers, we often do not get direct feedback on how students are understanding a particular work, and these sorts of exercises can help us revise content to improve student comprehension. It is interesting how often I discover that students are getting something different out of my material than I expected.

Strategic scaffolds

Students can also benefit from strategic scaffolds that guide them in completing an activity. Instead of just asking for a paper of a specific length, the instructor can specify the structure of the paper with instructions such as "Provide an introduction that covers... [or] provide a summary of the author's two main points on..." (Ifenthaler 2012). These questions help track the students' thinking through a process.

Another option is to provide a step-by-step guide to a process. For instance, when given a physics problem, students can be told: "First determine which of the conservation of energy principles applies to the problem. Then..." In this case, students are starting at the right place and using the correct process to work through the problem, just as we were given the correct process to make our canoe paddles.

This exercise also helps make student thinking visible. Often, faculty only see the product of student work, and thus cannot locate the error in the process that led to that product. For instance, a chemistry instructor might find that a student's problem is in identifying the correct principle to apply to the situation rather than in doing the math wrong on a formula. With this knowledge, the instructor knows what to work on with that student. Strategic scaffolding also cultivates students' metacognition about their own thinking process, and self-awareness of one's own thinking process has been identified as one of the most important drivers of learning.

Of course, the degree of scaffolding depends upon the level of student competence. Any assignment assumes some prior knowledge on the part of the student. The goal is to set the scaffolding just above this baseline to move the student up to the next level.

The instructor could also start the course with quite a bit of scaffolding, or scaffold at a fairly low conceptual level, and then gradually diminish the scaffolding or move it to a higher level so that it is always just above the students' current understanding. In this way, the instructor gradually draws the students up in skill level. Used to help advance students' thinking, scaffolding can be one of the most effective tools in an instructor's teaching toolbox.

References

Hannafin, M., S. Land, and K. Oliver. "Open Learning Environments: Foundations, Methods, and Models. In *Instructional-Design theories and models: A new paradigm of instructional theory*, edited by C. M. Reigeluth, vol. 2; 115–140. Mahwah, NJ: Lawrence Erlbaum Associates, 1999.

Ifenthaler, D. "Determining the Effectiveness of Prompts for Self-Regulated Learning in Problem-Solving Scenarios." *Educational Technology & Society* 15, no. 1 (2012), 38–52.

Reprinted from *Online Classroom*, July 2016.

Designing Online Learning to Spark Intrinsic Motivation

by Rebecca A. Zambrano, Edgewood College

The word "motivation" comes from a root that means "to move," and really, motivation is about what moves us to begin something or to persist in a situation—in this case, a learning situation. Motivation is a driving force. It can be considered an external driving force, something that motivates us from the outside, or a psychological force that compels us toward an action or a goal from the inside.

Extrinsic motivation—such as money or job security as motivators—is reward-based. We're moved to do something or persist because we want a reward of some kind that will come from completing the task. Intrinsic motivation is different. Curiosity, love of learning, the ability to use new knowledge and apply it to one's own goals: all of these are things that are intrinsically motivating to people. They're motivating because they're enjoyable, or because they satisfy an internal psychological desire.

Studies by Deci and Ryan have shown that intrinsic motivation tends to produce much deeper and more sustained engagement and learning than extrinsic motivation. And these studies have been followed up by many other studies that tend to have similar results.

Deci's 1996 book, *Why We Do What We Do: Understanding Self-Motivation*, includes a theory called self-determination theory, based on three categories of intrinsic motivation that the author claims are universal to all human beings. He argues that these three categories (competence, connection, and autonomy) are actually needs that all of us have to meet in our lives in order to experience our optimal potential as humans.

When all three of these needs are met, according to self-determination theory, we sustain our desire to keep learning. We sustain our desire to produce, to keep producing, be creative, give our time and energy to others, and, in general, increase and sustain our desire to live all the roles that we play in our lives to the best of our ability. But when one of these three needs is not met in some area, our motivation may suffer.

So in any learning situation, the student would, ideally, have all three needs met in order to want to sustain that learning over time without the need for the reward of money or grades or some other extrinsic motivator.

Looking at practical applications of the theory, one of the ways to think about this is that each student has a unique motivational profile of underlying desire and drives; as an instructor, getting to know students well can often make obvious what the main motivators are for particular students. Most students want to get a good grade, but it is the intrinsic motivators, such as the need to gain competence in a course or the need to have a sense of choice or a sense of directing their own learning to some degree or another, that motivates students to succeed.

Each student will have a different mix of those needs. It's often true, for example, that when professionals, as opposed to traditional students, come into an online class, their need to connect and network with others in the online format may not be as strong, and their need may be really more about gaining competence.

It is important for instructors to ask questions and reach out to students in order to learn more about their own specific motivational profiles. And, of course, if we were to ask them, "What is your motivational profile?" they probably wouldn't have a clue what to say. But questions about what they most liked or enjoyed about the learning in a particular assignment, what aspect of the assignment they didn't enjoy, or what was challenging for them—the answers to these questions give clues to their particular motivational profiles.

Not only can that help direct the learning in that course, but that feedback can be used in a redesign of a course later on. Before designing or improving an online course, ask some core questions: Why do people want to take the course? What is it that students are coming to class to gain? Are they there to learn skills? Are they there to tap into the creative potential of others who are working to solve complex issues in their workplaces?

Sometimes it's fair to assume that students want connectedness with others, but in a research class in a doctoral program, they may really want mentorship from the instructor of that class and not seek so much interaction with others. So, again, asking these questions can help in designing the most motivating kinds of assignments for the courses that you teach. It's also true though that even if an instructor has a very good understanding of the particular student population, there will be diversity within each course. So it is important to design with that in mind. Create a mix of assignments that recognizes the diversity of motivational profiles of students in all courses and include a choice of assignments where possible.

Developmental assignments

The idea behind a developmental assignment is that it helps students gain mastery over time at increasing levels of depth. For example, at the beginning of a course, students might be provided with a difficult case scenario that they have very little ability to solve or to analyze, but that they will have an increasing ability to solve or analyze over time. They revisit that same scenario a couple of weeks after the start of the course and write a whole new response or a whole new analysis that includes the learning that they have already done up to that point. Depending on the assignment and the level of complexity, students might revisit that case scenario three times, or it could be every week during the course.

But the key is for students to watch their own learning and ability grow over time. Which of Deci's three motivational needs would that apply to? Let's revisit those three needs. One is competence, one is relatedness with others, and one is autonomy or freedom. This developmental type of assignment meets the need for competence, as students are watching their abilities grow over time if they are successful.

In illustrating their abilities, students are also able to meet their need for autonomy. There are also ways to *add* autonomy to an assignment like this. When students have a choice, for example, in how they're going to present their increasing levels of skill, it can help with autonomy.

The developmental assignment can also increase the students' sense of belonging and relatedness. If, for example, they share their final analysis with others in the course, or maybe their halfway through analysis, or they seek support from others in the course, that could also meet the need for relatedness.

These categories are not always clear-cut, and that's not a bad thing. They're really there to help instructors think about how to increase the level of intrinsic motivation in their assignments.

The key to the developmental assignment is that students are revisiting in greater depth or complexity over time. They're revisiting the same content, to analyze it or discuss it and pull it apart, or maybe to add knowledge over time.

Autonomy

There are many ways to allow students to guide aspects of their learning, and very clearly meeting one of the needs that Ryan and Deci identify: the need for autonomy. One way to do so would be to invite students to create evaluation criteria for an assignment and offer their suggestions for criteria for a rubric. Students very much appreciate being given the chance to determine parts of how they're going to be evaluated.

Giving students a choice about what sections or chapters to cover also provides autonomy, as does allowing them to choose the exam format—for example, multiple choice versus essay.

There is more than one way to help students become free. Freedom can mean giving students more choice of what to do, or how to do it inside of our classrooms. But freedom can also mean freeing up our perspectives, and one way to do so is to examine multiple perspectives on the same topic.

Recognizing a lack of motivation

Some students do not come into class feeling as if their voices are valuable to the learning community. This can be true for a variety of reasons. In some cases, it may be because the content is so new to them that they don't really feel that they have a lot to add. In other cases, students may come in to a course with a language background that isn't standard English or doesn't match the academic English that's being used in the course. I think that can make some students very silent in our class discussion forums, at least initially.

In cases like this, how might an instructor intervene?

One of the clearest indicators of a lack of motivation is a lack of participation. In the online classroom, quality of communication can be quite important. If an instructor only uses the word count feature of the LMS, a lack of motivation can be easily missed, as students can obviously write a lot and not say very much in a discussion forum.

An early indicator is a student missing in action or typing just short little posts that lack much thought. When that happens, it's important to immediately contact the student by email or even phone. This can be a wakeup call, but the idea is definitely not to scare them. It's to have a supportive conversation and to remind the student of the shared goals of the class.

Adapted from the Magna Online Seminar presentation, *Designing Online Learning to Spark Intrinsic Motivation.*

Online Discussion Strategies That Create Community

by Maryellen Weimer, Penn State Berks

One of the biggest complaints about online courses is that students feel disconnected. They don't know the teacher or fellow students in the class. In online courses, teachers regularly use discussion to make connections with and between students. In a survey of over 350 faculty, 95 percent used discussion as a tool and 87 percent required student participation in online exchanges.

In their 2014 paper, deNoyelles, Zydney, and Chen used a "Community of Inquiry" framework for their exploration-specific strategies that can be used to build community through discussion in online courses. "The purpose of this paper is to discuss specific strategies that have been proven through empirical research to support online CoIs (Communities of Inquiry)" (155). They note that the literature on online discussion is voluminous, but to be included in their review, "the study had to have taken place in a fully online, higher education setting, utilized text-based asynchronous discussion, focused on the influence of a specific strategy, employed at least one direct research measure . . . and been peer reviewed" (155). They retrieved 220 potential studies, but only 36 met their criteria.

The Community of Inquiry model proposes three essential elements needed to make an educational experience successful: social presence, cognitive presence, and teacher presence. The authors explore the role of these elements and the strategies that can be used online to support them.

Social presence
    "One comment often heard from online instructors and students is

the loss of human touch in a fully online course" (deNoyelles, Zydney, and Chen 2014, 155). How do instructors go about creating a positive and supportive environment when students are not physically connected? Based on their review of the literature, the authors recommend two strategies: instructor modeling of social presence and required and graded discussions. They suggest that online instructors be personal in their communications with students. They should use students' names, express humor, and introduce relevant personal stories.

Research does not establish that social presence causes learning. Its power lies more in creating a climate that makes learning more likely to occur. Students build interpersonal connections when they interact with each other, which is the justification for requiring participation in these exchanges. Research indicates that when those discussions count for between 10 and 20 percent of the student's grade, the number of messages students post increases and their sense of classroom community is heightened. Interestingly, increasing the grade percentage to 25 to 35 percent garners no further benefits.

Cognitive presence

The problem that needs to be addressed here is the frequent failure of online discussions to go beyond idea exploration. "Students may be exchanging information and ideas, [but] they are rarely connecting and expanding on ideas, or applying new ideas to other contexts" (156). This can also be a problem in face-to-face discussions when students share their ideas without responding to the contributions of others. The authors cite research documenting that the prompts teachers use to promote online interaction can play an important role.

deNoyelles, Zydney, and Chen report, "Discussion prompts that inherently guide students to progress through the phases of cognitive presence were more successful in eliciting integration and resolution" (157). The cognitive phases referenced here include identification of an issue, the exchange of ideas and information about the issue, the connection of those ideas, and their application to new ideas. "Select a discussion prompt that encourages structured interaction and critical thinking, while also supporting the specific learning objectives" (161).

The prompts are important, and so are the facilitation methods used. "We argue it is not the mere presence of a facilitator that is effective, but rather the techniques employed" (158). For example, they recommend that teachers sometimes take a "challenging stance" by highlighting different viewpoints and asking for responses to those.

Teaching presence

Here one of the issues is the amount of time teacher facilitation of online discussions can take. If teachers are providing feedback to individual students and actively participating in the discussion, the time investment can be huge. And then there's the ongoing question of how much instructors should participate in online discussions. Research documents that teacher presence is the "backbone" (159) of creating community, which makes these important issues.

Among the authors' recommendations is the provision of "prompt but modest instructor feedback" (159). Multiple interventions by the instructor in online discussions do not lead to increases in student interaction. In fact, the research reveals that modest instructor feedback encourages students to take more ownership of the discussion, which increases the number of student-to-student exchanges. They also recommend the use of peer facilitators, as students may feel more comfortable in discussions led by peers.

Peer discussion leaders post more messages than do teachers, research has shown. However, the authors point out that peer facilitators will likely need specific instruction on what techniques they should use. Sometimes it helps to assign students facilitator roles such as discussion starter and wrapper (the role of summarizing an exchange).

Research also shows positive benefits of what the authors describe as "protocol prompts," which are "a structured method of having discussions by establishing a well-defined goal, clear roles, rules for interactions, and specific deadlines for posting" (160). Teachers might also consider providing audio or video feedback. Software makes it possible for teachers to verbally comment on a discussion exchange and post that feedback on a discussion board or send it via email. Students then get to hear the instructor, and additional messages are conveyed by tone of voice.

This helpful piece of scholarship tackles some of the challenges presented by online environments, suggesting research-tested strategies that have been shown to improve discussions and increase the sense of community in online courses.

Reference

deNoyelles, A., J. M. Zydney, and B. Chen. "Strategies for Creating a Community of Inquiry through Online Asynchronous Discussions." *Journal of Online Learning and Teaching*, 10, no. 1 (2014): 153–165.

Reprinted from *Online Classroom*, January 2015.

CHAPTER 3

•

Managing Challenging Behavior in the Online Classroom

A Proactive Approach to Promoting Civility in the Online Classroom

by Rob Kelly

Each time Joyce Johnston teaches an online course, she asks her students to select the characteristic that is most important in their online interactions. Invariably, students choose "respect." They want the learning environment to be civil, and Johnston, an English instructor at George Mason University, devotes the first week and a half of her class to promoting civility and reinforces it throughout the course.

Johnston recommends the following strategies to promote a civil online learning environment:

Model civility

"I am aggressively polite. I try to be a good model constantly. I always try to take a positive point of view and not criticize unless I have a positive suggestion to make," Johnston says.

Require each student to post a mug shot

Johnston herself and each student in her courses must include a photo—not an avatar—in his or her profile. Including a photo in the profile means that it will accompany each posting within the password-protected learning management system. "The fact that every time someone responds to a person, he or she is looking at a face has made a real difference in the class atmosphere," Johnston says.

Students don't experience the disassociation that often occurs in online communication. That relative anonymity can encourage incivility, "but when they see they're hurting a real human being, it's amazing how much more reluctant they become to do damage," Johnston says.

Use narration

Johnston uses Audacity (*audacity.sourceforge.net/*) to create narration throughout the course. The course orientation, in particular, lays the groundwork for a civil learning environment. Each study unit has its oral introduction, and each student essay is returned with an oral response that explains the grading, praises successes, and makes recommendations for improvement. "As our composition director said, I become the voice in their heads," Johnston explains.

Engage students on the topic of civility

The first week and a half of Johnston's courses is devoted to civility. "I teach a required course, so I can't afford to load anything they have to have for graduation in the first week and a half while students are still dropping and adding, but I would do it even if I were teaching an elective," she says.

An important exercise at the beginning of the course is a series of questions that students respond to in a blog. For instance, students are required to respond to the following question, created by J.D. Stemwedel: "Are there particular issues for which you have no realistic expectation that it's possible to discuss them civilly either online, offline, or both? What are they, and why do you think discussing them civilly is so hard?"

The purpose of this exercise is not to provide insights to the instructor—Johnston knows that the most frequent response is religion. The point of the question is to get students to be aware of potential controversial issues and to make an extra effort to be respectful when discussing these issues.

In addition to the first required question, Johnston requires that students also answer three more of Stemwedel's five questions in the blog:

- "Describe your experience with online interactions in different venues that are important to you, like Facebook, LinkedIn, and Twitter. How do users respond differently in these different environments? In what ways do you adjust your own persona and responses to accommodate the medium?"
- "What are the prospects for successful coalition-building when the differences include not respecting other people's feelings and/or prioritizing one's own insulation against feeling bad above everything else?"
- "What are the prospects for successful coalition-building across fairly significant differences (which might include differences in preferred level of politeness or civility)?"
- "What does it mean to be on the same team, at least from the point of view of feeling like we're entitled to expect a certain level of regard or kind of treatment from each other?"

- "What do we mean by 'we' in discussions of online civility?"
- "As they discuss and see each other's faces, they begin to bond without even knowing it," Johnston says.

Johnston also assigns readings about civility by P. M. Forni and John Suler during this time. In addition, she provides content from presentations she has conducted on the topic and has students take a netiquette quiz developed by Virginia Shea (*www.albion.com/netiquette/netiquiz.html*).

Embed civility exercises in group work and assessment

During the first week and a half, students also begin working in groups of three to assemble a wiki of resources within their fields. Students in each group decide how they will meet, and then do an exercise on how they will divide the work, how they will check in with each other, and what to do if a group member doesn't meet the group's expectations. This is a "civility exercise in disguise," Johnston says. "If somebody doesn't function, what steps do you take to try to get that person to function? At what point do you cut that person loose so you don't go down in flames as well? And how do you do that civilly?"

When the group finishes its wiki, each group member evaluates the functioning of the group. Group members evaluate themselves and each other and comment on civility issues or group compatibility. Getting feedback from each other serves as a "reality check," Johnston says. "Sometimes it's a matter of perception as to who thinks who did how much."

Johnston also has students write an essay on how they can improve their work in groups, as they will work in two more, different groups during the course.

One group activity is peer review. Offering and receiving feedback from peers can create the potential for incivility. To reduce this potential, Johnston recommends that each student cue reviewers: What are you working on? What do you feel your weaknesses are? What do you want your reviewers to help you with? This helps peers provide targeted comments. "It controls the dialogue... Everybody loves that because readers have defined tasks and know that they are being helpful," Johnston says.

Using these techniques has nearly eliminated incivility in Johnston's online courses. If a student adopts a less-than-civil tone in a post or message, Johnston replies, "I treat you with unfailing courtesy and expect you to treat me the same way. If you have real questions or concerns, please rewrite this in a way that we can discuss it. Then I'll be glad to respond."

Reprinted from *Online Classroom*, January 2014.

How Do I Get Students to Come to Class Prepared?

by J. Robert Gillette, University of Kentucky, and Lynn Gillette, Nicholls State University

Why do students come to class unprepared? Because teachers tend to lecture on the material, and students find it most efficient to let them lecture first and then read later. But if your students came to class prepared, would they acquire a deeper understanding of the material?

What I've heard for years from teachers is, "If I could only get my students to come prepared, then I could rock and roll in class." But how do you get students prepared? Rather than finding a solution, this quandary typically comes down to a faculty member bemoaning the current state of students. But it *is* possible: you can get your students to come to class prepared.

If they came prepared, how would that change the way you teach? Once students come prepared, teachers have to adjust to that fact. We can get our students to come to class prepared, but it requires a different course design.

Let's compare the traditional model of teaching to an interactive model of teaching. We have class time, we have student alone time, and we have teacher alone time. And for the aspects of learning, we have first exposure, higher-order reasoning like critical thinking, and then we have teacher response time.

In the traditional model, first exposure to material is done during class. The teacher lectures on the material. The student receives it for the first time. In student alone time, we send the students off by themselves to do critical thinking on problem sets or homework where they have to apply, analyze, or synthesize the material without the instructor's help at that time. And then in teacher response, the instructor gets back the homework or problem sets, and grades them one by one by one by one like a cottage industry, if you will.

With the interactive model, we change up when we do first exposure, higher-order reasoning, and then teacher response.

With first exposure, we direct students by giving them a guided reading assignment and have them gain the knowledge of first exposure by themselves. Then, when they come to class, we're all together to do higher-order reasoning like applying, synthesizing, evaluating, and critical thinking. And we do it all *during* class time.

When you do a problem set in the traditional model, students may be working on the problem at 2 a.m. when the instructor is dead asleep. But in class time, when you've got students working on higher-order reasoning at 2 o'clock in the afternoon, they've got other students and instructors in class to guide them. So in the interactive model, we're doing the heavy lifting of critical thinking in class when students can work with each other, and instructors can guide them through any troubles that they're having with the problem.

Then with teacher response, instead of grading all these problems one by one by one, we can sit during class time and guide the students, giving them feedback on what's wrong; we can do all the problems at one time or at least do lots of them at one time. So it's more efficient in terms of responding. Then in the interactive model with teacher alone time, the teacher can come up with learning activities to sink the students into deeper understanding of the material during class and also come up with activities and questions to guide their reading for the first exposure.

This interactive model uses class preparation assignments and a definitional grading system. The class preparation assignments are guided writing assignments that give students something to read and questions to keep in mind while they're reading. This guides them and serves as a basis for discussion in class when we come back together. Class preparation assignments are pass/fail. Once you receive them from students, you can determine pretty quickly whether somebody's done the work.

To earn a class preparation assignment (CPA) credit, a student must:

1. Show a good-faith effort on every question
   First, students have to show a good-faith effort on every question. The response doesn't have to be perfect—this is first exposure. But students *must* make a good-faith effort in answering every question.

2. Submit one copy before discussion
   Students must bring two copies of their answers to class, one to turn in and one to refer to during class.

3. Participate in in-class learning

Students have to attend class to be able to get credit for class preparation assignments. And students must successfully complete class preparation assignments and pass all quizzes and exams in order to get a passing grade.

CPAs change the way we teach

Once students come prepared, instructors need to teach accordingly. Students are ready to go, so the instructor must use active learning strategies to seek higher-level critical thinking and informed opinions on what students have already read.

Now that students are coming to class prepared, instructors must change the way they teach. A straight lecture will cause students to lose motivation. Students have read the material. They've come to class. They know something about it. This means teaching strategies must change. Applying active learning strategies can help facilitate this change:

- *Make space and time for student voices.* In a certain sense, college students are like teenagers. They're talked at and talked to quite often, instead being respected and asked for their opinions. I think it shows a lot of respect to students to have a class where instructors talk less, students talk more, and everyone takes part in an informed discussion. Not only are CPAs used to flesh out what students think, we can also use them to sink students into deeper understanding. So we as instructors come in and say, "Okay, they're informed." We want to hear from them, but we also want to train them to have skills that show they can understand high-level thinking.
- *Use cooperative learning.* Group work, workshops, and other active learning strategies lead students to engaging in deeper learning and really critically thinking about the material. A think, pair, share strategy, where the instructor throws out a problem, gives students about a minute to sit and think or write about it, and then asks them to pair up and share what they're talking about, gets about 50 percent of the class talking about the class material to one another and responding to each other with feedback. This approach gives space to introverts by giving them time to think. In this way, you've given them time to talk to other people, instead of allowing extroverts to dominate the conversation.

Conclusion

Having students come to class prepared is a course design issue. Solving this problem involves setting up incentives and constraints that the students will respond to. If you use the definitional grading system and the class preparation system, you'll get your students to come prepared, and you can then focus much more on deep analytical thinking. It's not the only way to get students prepared, but it's a very effective way to get students prepared.

Adapted from the Magna 20-Minute Mentor presentation, *How Do I Get Students to Come to Class Prepared?*

Meet Students Where They Are

by Rob Kelly

Valerie Powell, assistant professor of art at Sam Houston State University, decided to supplement her face-to-face courses using technology to extend the classroom and provide opportunities for students who are not comfortable speaking up in the face-to-face environment. Rather than demanding that students interact using a specific tool, however, she offers options "to meet students where they are."

Powell created a Facebook page for the Workshop in Art Studio and History (WASH) program, an immersive nine-credit "art boot camp" that includes principles of design and theory. In general, her students, mostly first-year and transfer students, are comfortable interacting online but not necessarily within a learning management system. This is why, in addition to using Blackboard, she uses social media, particularly Facebook, to get students to interact online.

Powell likes Blackboard, but her students don't. They use it mainly to check their grades. "They just don't seem comfortable with that particular tool. They're freshmen. It's very new to them, whereas they've been using Facebook forever," Powell says.

One requirement of the program is for students to critique each other's work in progress. They can post images of their work for feedback in Blackboard or on Facebook. "It gets them in the habit of learning how to document their work and gets them comfortable asking questions," Powell says. "I have them post an image and ask a question, such as, 'What can I do to improve this?' Then they are required to comment on each other's work.

"The first time I did this, I thought it might help a few people," Powell relates. "Instead, I found that there was complete participation. They were making comments and using vocabulary from the textbook. I'd never heard a lot of these students talk before, and they were making smart comparisons and were confident in their opinions. It was such a wakeup call for me. This is a really good platform for them. They're already comfortable with it."

The Facebook page is an open page. Former students, professors, and even the general public can comment on students' work. Posting images of their work also gives students the opportunity to gain experience photographing their work, and "it's a nice way to make them aware that they are making their work for an audience," Powell says.

This online forum provides opportunities for every student to participate. "It's really important to allow everyone to have an opportunity to participate. I found that creating online discussions really allows those [introverted] students to have a voice, because many of them are comfortable on Facebook. They tend to have conversations that extend beyond the classroom in a way that I don't think happens if it's just a traditional discussion," Powell notes.

For those who are not comfortable posting to a public Facebook page, Powell offers the option of posting their work to Blackboard, which is not open to the public. Most students choose to post in Facebook. "I found that a lot of students are very excited to have that conversation in a place online where other people can join in, especially professors they'll have in the future," Powell says. "[These students] really like to live out loud. They're very public. They want everybody to know what they're doing and generally seem to like being on Facebook and having their images on there. There's a sense of pride, whereas on Blackboard, it's very closed. Students have said, 'When we had to post stuff on Blackboard it felt like an assignment. On Facebook, it feels like I was doing it because I wanted to do it.'"

In addition to Facebook, Powell uses a WordPress home page for the program and encourages the use of tools such as chat and other social media like Pinterest and Twitter. "If it were up to me, I'd create this happy little place where we'd all be on one website," Powell says, noting that managing the online portion of the course would likely be easier if the online components were in one place. "But I think it's important to be more focused on the needs of the students and the best ways to get them to perform at their best, rather on than how I can make this easier on me."

Powell recommends implementing the use of social media incrementally. "Rather than redesigning your entire curriculum so you have this epic online component that's going to change everyone's lives, why not create one smaller project that has elements that encourage students to interact online, whether it's research or critique?" she suggests.

"Part of being an effective instructor is being open to suggestions for new tools and strategies. How can I ask my students to take risks and try things beyond their comfort zone if I'm not willing to do that as well?" Powell asks.

Reprinted from *Online Classroom*, April 2014.

Do Online Students Cheat More on Tests?

by Maryellen Weimer, Penn State Berks

Do online students cheat more on tests? A lot of faculty worry that they do. Given the cheating epidemic in college courses, why wouldn't students be even more inclined to cheat in an unmonitored exam situation? Add to that how tech-savvy most college students are. Many know their way around computers and software better than their professors do. Several studies report that the belief that students cheat more on online tests is most strongly held by faculty who've never taught an online course. Those who *have* taught online are less likely to report discernible differences in cheating between online and face-to-face courses. But those are faculty perceptions, not hard, empirical evidence.

In a study designed to look more closely at this perception, researcher Beck correctly notes that research on cheating abounds, and it addresses a wide range of different questions and issues (2014). Faculty have been asked how often they think cheating occurs and what they do about it when it happens. Students have been asked whether they or their peers would cheat, given a certain set of circumstances. Students have also been asked how often they cheat, how often they think their peers do, and whether they report cheating. The problem with much of this descriptive research is that it summarizes perceptions—what faculty and students think and have experienced with respect to cheating. And this, in part, explains why the results vary widely (studies report cheating rates anywhere between 9 and 95 percent) and are sometimes contradictory and therefore inconclusive.

A different approach

Beck opted to take a different approach in her study of cheating in online and face-to-face classes. She used a statistical model to predict academic dishonesty in testing. It uses measures of "human capital" (GPA and class rank, for example) to predict exam scores. "This model proposes that the more human capital variables explain variation in examination scores, the more likely the examination scores reflect students' abilities and the less likely academic dishonesty was involved in testing" (Beck 2014, 65). So if a student has a high GPA and is taking a major course, the assumption is that the student studied, cares about the course, and therefore earned the grade. But if a student has a low GPA and doesn't care about the course, yet ends up with a high exam score, chances are the student cheated. It's an interesting method that involves a good deal more complexity than described here. The article includes full details of the assumptions and how the model was developed and used.

The study looked at exam scores (midterms and finals, all containing the same questions) of students in three sections of the same course. One section contained an online unmonitored exam, another was an online hybrid section with a monitored exam (students took this exam in a testing center facility), and the third was a face-to-face section with the test monitored by the instructor. In the online unmonitored section, questions were randomized so that each student received a unique test. Online students could not exit or restart an exam once they began taking it. The exam was presented one question at a time; students could not move backward through the questions; and the exam was automatically submitted after 70 minutes, the time allowed in the other two formats. Students in all sections were warned not to engage in cheating.

"Based on the results in this study, students in online courses with unmonitored testing are no more likely to cheat on an examination than students in hybrid and face-to-face courses using monitored testing, nor are students with low GPAs more likely to enroll in online courses" (Beck 2014, 72). That last comment addresses a critique of online classes: some have suggested that because students who had not taken an online course reported that they thought it would be easier to cheat in online courses, students with lower GPAs might be motivated to take online courses. There were only 19 students in the online course in this study, but across these three sections, GPA did not differ significantly.

When using this interesting model to predict cheating, there was no evidence that it occurred to a greater degree in the unmonitored tests given in the online course. That's the good news. The bad news: "There is ample opportunity for cheating across all types of course delivery modes, which has been demonstrated through decades of research" (Beck 2014, 73). In other words, we still have a problem—it just isn't more serious in online courses, based on these results.

Reference

Beck, V. "Testing a Model to Predict Online Cheating—Much Ado about Nothing." *Active Learning in Higher Education* 15, no. 1 (2014): 65–75.

Reprinted from *Online Classroom*, April 2014.

Advice for Dealing with Stressed and Anxious Students

by Rob Kelly

Ken Einhaus, a project manager at the Center for Applied Research Solutions, offers dos and don'ts for dealing with online learners exhibiting a variety of mental health crises, including the following recommendations for dealing with stressed and anxious students:

- Listen sincerely.
- Provide appropriate reassurance and a safe and quiet environment until the symptoms decrease.
- Be calm, clear, and directive.
- Encourage the student to get help by talking with a counselor, attending a stress management workshop, or consulting various online resources.
- Don't minimize the severity of the student's symptoms or perceived threat.
- Don't take responsibility for the student's emotional state.
- Don't overwhelm the student with ways to "fix" his or her situation.

Reference

Einhaus, Ken. "Responding to Difficult or Distressed Online Students: Mental Health Assessment and Referrals." Accessed September 22, 2014. *http://cccstudentmentalhealth.org/docs/CCCSMHP-Online-Students-MH-Assessments-Referrals.pdf.*

Reprinted from *Online Classroom,* October 2014.

How to Handle Distressed or Disruptive Online Learners

by Rob Kelly

Over the past several decades, advances in medicine and therapy have allowed more people with mental health challenges to function as productive members of society, and to pursue higher education. The percentage of students receiving treatment for mental illness in college has risen from 9 percent in 1994 to 17 percent in 2000, and was 24.4 percent in 2012. The passage of the Affordable Care Act and the Mental Health Parity and Addiction Equity Act have further improved access to mental health care, enabling more people with mental illness to stay on track to improve their economic prospects through higher education, meaning more instructors are encountering more students with mental health challenges in the online classroom. If the benefits of higher education are to be afforded to all, instructors must learn to recognize the signs of common mental health issues and to know their role in supporting online learners and their classmates with mental and emotional challenges and disabilities.

According to the National Alliance on Mental Illness (NAMI), "mental illness" is an umbrella term that includes a host of conditions that cause severe disturbances in thinking, feeling, functioning, and relating to others. Like physical health and illness, all of us have mental health to maintain, and mental illness is surprisingly common but underreported. Half of us (46 percent) will experience mental illness in some form within our lifetime, including anxiety or depression. One in four (26 percent) experience at least one diagnosable disorder each year, and one in 17 (6 percent) experience a seriously debilitating mental disability each year. Stressors common to the college environment can exacerbate the symptoms of mental illness and can create short-term difficulties for students, including those without chronic diagnoses. How students cope can make or break their academic future. A student who experiences a difficult breakup or whose psychiatric medications are disrupted may lose his or her scholarship if they allow their GPA to fall during a depressive period, and lose the ability to pursue higher education in the future.

Despite this growing need to know how to work with online learners experiencing mental and emotional challenges, there has not been much written on the topic. Moreover, higher education institutions generally do not have the resources and policies in place for online students to the extent that they do for their on-campus students, says Ken Einhaus, project manager at the Center for Applied Research Solutions, who helps manage technical assistance and training for the California Community Colleges Student Mental Health Program (*http://cccstudentmentalhealth.org*).

The role of the online instructor is to be aware of the issues that affect the academic success of his or her students and to provide the support they need—not to serve as a therapist. One of the challenges of recognizing mental illness in one's online students is the lack of face-to-face contact. A lack of visual cues or verbal tone means instructors need to look for other indicators, such as:

- Not logging into the class on a regular basis
- Lack of participation in the discussion board
- Missed assignments
- Decrease in quality of work
- Not taking advantage of opportunities to retake quizzes for a better grade
- Undeliverable emails
- Poor quality of postings
- Rambling postings indicating a threat to self or others
- Difficulty following written directions
- Writing that could indicate mental turmoil

When an instructor observes two or more of these indicators, it's important to express concern and ask what's going on. For example, an instructor might write, "I've noticed that the quality of your work took a sudden dive three weeks ago. Is there something I can help you with? Is there something going on?" Then, if necessary, the instructor can refer the student to the appropriate resources on campus or online (see the list of resources below).

It can be an awkward and unpleasant exchange, but, Einhaus says, it's better to offer and get a response of "No, thank you. I'm fine," than it is to not get the student needed help for fear of offending him or her. "A well-intentioned offer of assistance will be more easily forgiven than the consequences of somebody needing help and not getting it," he says. "I encourage teachers to take risks that way. Indicate that your door will be open to talk to students about any stress related to carrying out their assignments. That is a professional way to indicate that you are available to students to communicate their issues. But you want to be making observations within your realm as a teacher."

When faced with a potential mental health crisis, it's important to know what resources are available to you as an instructor. Specifically, Einhaus recommends:

- Know the mental health referral policies and protocols of your institution, and know whom to contact.
- Be familiar with mental health resources that are available online.
- When you observe signs of distress, communicate with the student privately via chat, telephone, or email.
- Be mindful of any background knowledge you have of the student from the first-week introductions.
- Listen carefully and try to understand the student's perspective without agreeing or disagreeing. Identify the student's concerns as well as your own.
- Keep a written record of your concerns and interventions, as well as the student's responses.
- Share your concerns with your institution's behavioral intervention team (BIT) if it has one. BITs are groups of key staff and personnel who convene on a regular or as-needed basis to discuss incidents of concern.

"BITs are basically the way for teachers to get help because teachers are not going to have this training. Teachers can be trained to conduct brief assessments, do standard referrals, and understand what mental health problems look like, but they're not ultimately going to, and should not be expected to, provide therapy," Einhaus says. "Ideally the campus would have some kind of system for that, and it wouldn't be all on the teacher. The teacher would just have a smooth handoff. I think ultimately that's going to happen. The problem in the interim will be the teachers who are teaching for institutions that don't provide mental health services to any degree, especially in an online setting. That's where we have to work around those problems. Hopefully, the teacher will have somebody with some psychological training on hand to know what that student needs [in order to] stay in the course."

The California Community Colleges Student Mental Health Program is funded by the voter-approved Mental Health Services Act (Prop. 63). It is one of several Prevention and Early Intervention Initiatives implemented by the California Mental Health Services Authority (CalMHSA), an organization of California counties working to improve mental health outcomes for individuals, families, and communities. For more information, visit www.calmhsa.org.

Reprinted from *Online Classroom*, October 2014.

Success Assured: How to Apply Classroom Management Skills to the Online Environment

by Jessica Harris and Sami Lange, Santa Rosa Junior College

As every instructor knows, whether it's shouting in class or shouting online, a student's rude or aggressive behavior can have unfortunate consequences in the classroom. Two online instructors decided to explore how face-to-face classroom management skills can translate to the online environment. Reviewing a series of community college courses, the authors identify four common disruptive behaviors and present a toolkit of proactive measures that instructors can use to facilitate a productive online learning environment.

Disruptive behavior

Disruptive student behavior such as laughter, outbursts, and foul language can prove a challenge even for an experienced instructor. While unanticipated behavior may require pulling a student aside for a private email or discussion, instructors can avoid much of this unpredictability by taking the time to establish credibility, authority, and expectations at the outset of the class.

An introduction forum is a popular first online assignment in which students share details about themselves and demonstrate familiarity with the class site. Why not use the forum as an opportunity to convey your credentials and model the language, tone, and type of critical thinking expected throughout the course? Think of the introduction forum as your first stop in reinforcing the online codes of conduct you will have already included in your syllabus and other introductory materials. Keep in mind that forums are also useful tools to call attention to good work. An early and well-considered reply to a student post can help nurture desired behaviors and promote communication among peers.

Student questions

Ever wake up to a flurry of emails from the same student each morning? In the face-to-face classroom, an instructor may pace the lesson to accommodate questions at predetermined points; however, in the online environment, students may (mistakenly!) think they have 24/7 instant messaging rights to contact the instructor. Again, proactive measures can help counteract this assumption. Providing office hours, online or otherwise, is a given. Consider designating particular days for responses to email inquiries; this approach not only assures students you will address concerns, but also allows them time to fully consider the material, avoiding premature questions.

Peer forums, such as Q&A or Tips & Tricks, can also help minimize duplicative inquiries (technical challenges, for example) and encourage the peer interaction and support typically seen outside the classroom. Some instructors offer extra credit for students who answer other students' questions on these boards (with instructor monitoring, of course). Finally, sending out a weekly email can act as a helpful reminder of the full range of tools and support available.

Lack of engagement

Have the opposite problem? Have your students checked out? A healthy volume and diversity of student participation contribute to a lively and dynamic class environment. When it comes to the seemingly apathetic student, the absence of body language and verbal cues can make it difficult to decipher the lack of motivation. While some students in the face-to-face classroom eagerly speak up in class, others may be more inclined to express themselves in small group discussions. The same is true in the online environment. While some students may appreciate the opportunity to express themselves in a public forum, others may be quicker to respond to activities such as a small group wiki project or a one-on-one peer review. Be sure to include varied materials, such as readings, videos, and interactive lessons or projects, that will address the diverse learning styles and interests of your students.

Late/incomplete assignments

"So… I can hand this stuff in any time before the course ends, right?" In the online environment, poor class attendance can make an appearance in the form of late assignments or incomplete coursework. Students may assume that online courses offer flexible deadlines or a lighter workload than do their face-to-face counterparts. Including language regarding anticipated workload, deadlines, and late assignments in a pre-class "welcome" email and syllabus can help enlighten misinformed students.

To reiterate these requirements, consider including this information as a standard addendum in a weekly email. Persistence will prevail! If you do decide to accept a late assignment (everyone can be a softie), reminding the student of the deadlines going forward can save aggravation and misunderstandings later down the line. However, what if a student's coursework is late simply due to the unanticipated technological savvy required by an online course? Again, highlighting the technological prerequisites, requirements, and resources in your introductory materials will go a long way to helping alleviate frustration on the parts of both students and instructors.

Last thoughts? It's an online class. Don't be invisible. Be known. Be real. Whether it's a funny line in a lesson or an email (isn't humor always a common denominator?) or feedback that highlights a specific detail in a student's work, establishing a personal connection is critical to engaging students in the online environment. When students feel relevant and connected, they contribute. Taking the time to think about how you can proactively help your students better navigate and interact with the online environment can be the key to supporting a productive and dynamic online classroom.

Reprinted from *Online Classroom*, March 2015.

How Can Course Design Help Prevent Online Cheating?

by Tom Tobin, Northeastern Illinois University

Think about how we usually try to detect and discourage cheating in face-to-face courses. Most of us have a sixth sense about work that doesn't seem right. Suddenly a freshman student starts using semicolons properly. Or there's a section in a paper spelled with British English—you know: *whilst* and color spelled with "o-u-r."

When we think about online assignments and courses, we usually go right to the major student writing assignments and online exams. But academic integrity starts long before students ever engage with the high-points, high-stakes parts of our courses.

My model has three levels, or three paths, that we can give our students for academic honesty. The first, and most basic, relationship we can have with our students is one of trust. We don't have to, and we shouldn't, send every little thing that they do for us through a plagiarism checker.

Trust

The strategy of trusting students tells them two important things: One, we expect honest behavior from them. And two, we're giving them some freedom in our courses.

The best trust mechanism is an honor code. At Georgia Tech, the honor code is emailed to every new student from the dean. Keep in mind that honor codes work best when they are everywhere. Students don't see them only at freshman orientation: faculty members put the honor code into their syllabi, on the front page of the online course shells, in the directions for every course assignment, and in the description of every test and quiz.

After we worked with faculty to implement this continual presence for the honor code, we've seen our academic dishonesty rates go down. The greatest decrease that we saw was in our online courses.

It's tempting to cheat due to factors like time pressure or having things not be clear and running out of time. The honor code helps students understand that the expectation is that they can talk to their professors if such factors arise, working out a better alternative to cheating that will support, instead of undermine, their learning.

It sets up a positive expectation of ethical behavior. And it gives students a behavior that they can use if they get in a bind and are tempted to cheat. Giving students an honor code that is both "here's what we expect you to do" and "here's what you can do if things go wrong" really moves the needle on academic integrity.

Now, more effective than honor code displays are sanction statements right at the point of need. Sanction statements are another form of trust. They tell students that honest conduct is expected and valued, what that honest conduct looks like, and what penalties exist for not following along (those are the sanctions themselves).

Sanction statements should be displayed wherever you want students to limit themselves in some way, like not using their books or notes. For example, a sanction statement in an online test might say "Question number one: By taking this online exam, I agree that I am the person who is supposed to be taking this exam. I don't have any outside help. I'm not using my textbook or my notes. I will honor the conditions of the exam. And I won't share the questions or the answers from this exam with anybody else."

Now, does this have any legal standing? Could you sue the student for sharing your exam with everybody else, say, in the fraternity or in the class? Probably not. At the same time, in your campus online integrity process, this statement has great weight. And it counts as evidence for students not doing what they're supposed to be doing, if it comes to that.

The better part of this, though, is that it shows students that you care that they're being academically honest. That will help reduce the number of students who are tempted to cheat in the first place. And from a faculty perspective, I hate doing the paperwork when students cheat. So I'd rather they don't cheat. Thus, this is a great strategy.

Now, skeptics might say, "Well, this doesn't prevent anyone from disobeying the sanction statement." But that's not the point. The point is to make students stop and think about the positive expectations for their own conduct. Research shows us that just reading and thinking about academic honesty significantly reduces the temptation to cheat.

A final strategy adds some teeth to the idea of trust; that's to use the honor code plus a typed response. As in this example, the first question of a quiz can be the honor code. In this case, the short answer field asks for the name of the student who agrees to abide by the honor code, who does so by keying his or her name.

Now, is that a legally binding agreement? Again, no. It does, though, require that students actually take an action to demonstrate their understanding of the trust we're giving them and makes them more likely to uphold it. The story here has to do with where else our students are being asked to key their name in. If you open a bank account; if you go to get a loan for a house; when you open all of the accounts that you have on Facebook, Instagram, or anywhere online and throughout life, you have to verify that you are who you are. Even when you install software on your computer, you have an End User License Agreement (the EULA) that most people just scroll to the bottom of and say "I accept."

What the sanction statement with the keyed-in name does is to get people to not just skip past the agreement but to actually focus on what they're signing, what they're saying they're going to do. That moves the needle on academic integrity quite a bit.

And that wraps up the idea of trust. Trust is the thing that we should do most often throughout every course that we teach online.

Verification

Now, beyond trust is verification. This is what most of us think of as an academic integrity strategy: the "catching cheaters" part of the package. Verifying what students are doing goes beyond just sending their papers to a plagiarism-checker service. Let's look at some verification methods and where you should use them in your online course shell.

Of course, the big databases like Turnitin and SafeAssign do have a role to play in catching dishonest behavior. They are very good at catching copying, since their databases scan the Internet, library databases, known cheat paper sites, and millions of already uploaded student submissions.

Use the big databases particularly for draft work or prep work, so students can see their own database reports and learn how to correct poor practices. This example is an especially revealing one:

My colleagues in the history department often had great big high-stakes papers due at the end of the semester. The underlying assumption was, well, these students are adults. They should be able to handle their own time. We're going to give them suggested milestones at the one-third, two-thirds, and then all-the-way-done parts of the course.

At about one-third, you should have a resource list together. About two-thirds through, you should have drafted your final paper. By the end of the course, you should have your final paper ready to turn in. And by the way, that final paper is worth 50 percent of your grade.

It's no surprise that my colleagues came to us saying, "Hey, people are cheating on these things." The paper was worth an awful lot of points. And there weren't ways for students to see if they were doing okay, or if they were on track as the course went along.

What we suggested, and what the instructors eventually implemented, was asking students to create their resource list and submit that to the professor for a check mark that they had done it. The professor would then put the resource list, along with some annotations and the student's summary of what they planned to use from the resources, through Turnitin, the plagiarism-checking service that our university subscribes to.

The students and the professor got back those reports, and for those students whose report results were high on the index of "this is copied," the professor was able to reach out to dig deeper. Oftentimes, the students themselves said, "Oh, wait, I didn't know that I needed to do something different here" or "I guess I need to be a little bit more original."

This meant it was a *learning* conversation rather than a *cheating* conversation. And because it happened before the students earned any points, there weren't any consequences; moreover, the students could recover from poor performance. The incidents of cheating on the final item went down dramatically.

Now, what if you don't have access to one of the big databases? An alternative is the poor professor's plagiarism database: your favorite search engine. The term "Google fishing" is even part of our lexicon these days.

Take a suspect passage. Plug it into the search engine. And voila, there's the source.

Of course, in order to go fishing, you have to be suspicious in the first place. So this is a useful double-check, not a solid strategy for overall detection.

You can see that in this case I've used Google. You can use any other search engine you like to come up with some pretty good hits on a suspect paper.

One of my challenges is deciding, "Should I be lenient with this student, or should I come down on him like a hammer?" Well, I think I should be lenient—because the suspect paper that got those strong hits I mentioned above was one of my own undergraduate papers. So academic integrity is definitely a learned skill. It's not something that we can assume our students are coming to us with. If I can get it, your students can get it.

What we don't often think of as a verification practice involves using the analytic data that the learning management system (LMS) provides us in order to check for dishonest behavior. For example, if most students in your course spend 45 minutes completing an online quiz and one student roars through in 10 minutes, that's cause to start asking a few questions.

For example, in my own educational technology graduate courses, I have an assignment where I ask students to work through a sample website that is a simulation of what it's like to be a student with a visual disability looking at a web page. For those students who spend more than 30 minutes trying to find information on this purposely difficult-to-access website, I know that they're probably giving it a good try.

I've had students go through in five minutes and get all the answers right—which, even as somebody who's used a screen reader a thousand times, I could never do. Those students are either people with visual disabilities who are actually using screen readers—and I've had a few of those—or they're people who got the answers from someone else. And I've had a few of those, too.

Using the analytics in your LMS is an easy double-check for time on task. Most learning management systems today can tell professors: How long did a student stay on this page? How many times did the student come back and look at it again? How long did the student take to answer this particular question on this particular quiz?"

Another tactic for verification is unique to online tests and quizzes. We can set limits for students in terms of the dates and times when tests are available. Be careful not to be so restrictive that some students cannot find time to take the assessment, though.

There are also third-party tools that restrict test-takers to using a special browser that disallows common actions like opening new computer windows, copying, and pasting.

In both of these cases, time limitations and using special browsers, these are technological limitations. We have to make sure that human limitations are also taken into account. For example, with my online tests and quizzes, I'll always make sure that they're available during the day on a weekday, in the evening on a weekday, and on at least one weekend day.

That might be more than we would offer our face-to-face students. And we don't want to open it up a whole week or two weeks, if the minimum amount of time we need to have it open is only perhaps two or three days. At the same time, for academic integrity, we want to make sure that we give students a good shot at taking the examination or quiz, and that we give them enough time to be able to do it.

My good rule of thumb is for you, the professor, to take your own test or quiz. Actually do it online. See how much time that takes you. Multiply that by one and a half. Then give your students that much time. If it took me 60 minutes to take my test or quiz, I'll give my students 90 minutes.

Again, the aim is not to prevent cheating—students can defeat restricted browsers by pulling out their mobile phones—but to underscore the importance of test security and the gravity of choosing to be dishonest. Use this kind of verification only for the big stuff that is worth the most course credit, usually the middle, term, and final examinations.

When we apply for credit cards, auto loans, or mortgages online, we usually have to prove that we are who we say we are. We answer questions about where we used to live, what car we used to drive, and how many teeth we had extracted after we got into a fight behind the high school when we were 17. No, I'm just kidding about that last one. I think.

This type of verification includes not only challenge questions like these, but also fingerprint scanning and other biometrics. You can probably also tell that this kind of verification is on the more expensive end of the spectrum from plagiarism databases and Google fishing. So use this only where the stakes are really high, like with online certification and licensing examinations.

Observation

The gold standard of all academic integrity methods is observation. If we can directly see the student as he or she is demonstrating the skill, we are most confident in their performance.

There are three kinds of observation. Even though we're talking about online tests and quizzes, face-to-face observation is still the most reliable anti-cheating strategy. Bring your students into a classroom or computer lab and have them take your online test or quiz under observed conditions.

This doesn't work for fully distance education courses where students are spread out geographically. But if you can bring students together for at least the high-stakes pieces of your course, like the final exam, it's the best way to observe them.

The next best thing is to set up proctoring agreements with other institutions, such as public libraries, other colleges and universities, and even workplace supervisors. Define the conditions you need for testing. Get the proctor to sign off for the observation. And then either pay that person a small stipend or offer reciprocal proctoring on your own campus for others.

A final form of observation takes advantage of the computerized nature of tests and quizzes. Third-party software and some learning management systems allow you to take continuous video, snap random camera shots, or record the keystrokes of test-takers. These methods are the most intrusive and should be used only for high-stakes assessments. In fact, none of the observation approaches are appropriate for everyday academic integrity needs. Where students are working together, starting processes, and doing everyday things like taking quizzes, allow them a measure of trust. For assessments, draft work, lab results, or anything that shouldn't be faked, make sure to verify that the students are doing authentic work and that they are respecting the conditions you've set for their work, as well. And for the times when students are playing for big points or high stakes, use a strategy for observing them as they demonstrate their skills.

By adopting this three-tiered approach to academic integrity, your online interactions with your students can focus on building a culture of credibility and honesty for your course. And you can catch cheaters, too.

Reprinted from *Online Classroom*, April 2015.

Five Ways to Help Students Succeed in the Online Classroom

by Amy Hankins, University of Phoenix

More and more students are flocking to the online classroom for the convenience of earning college credits from the comfort of their home. However, many of these students are ill-prepared for the dedication and discipline needed to be successful in the online environment. Often-times, students have misconceptions concerning the rigor of online courses, and they often underestimate the amount of time and discipline necessary to complete assignments, discussions, quizzes, and projects. Therefore, it is important for the instructor to set the tone of the course to help students succeed. So how do you help your students succeed in the online classroom?

1. **Provide detailed instructions and anticipate questions.** Ensure all instructions are easy to follow. Provide step-by-step instructions and ensure no detail is overlooked. Do not assume students will be able to read between the lines. Instead, provide students with every detail needed to complete the assignment, participate in discussions, navigate the course, etc. Consider the possible questions students might ask about the materials and answer them before students have an opportunity to ask. Provide these answers within the course instructions and course announcements.

2. **Post announcements.** Remain present in the course by posting announcements. At the very least, post an announcement each week to wrap up the previous week and let students know what to expect in the upcoming week. If possible, try to post at least two announcements per week. Announcements also provide an opportunity to do some housecleaning. Provide reminders, clarification, and overviews

to help engage and motivate students and help them see that you're involved in their learning.

3. **Provide examples and rubrics.** Again, to minimize questions and confusion, provide students with examples of the larger assignments in the course. If there will be an essay or a presentation, give students an example to show them how to do it. Quality examples from previous students in the course can be particularly helpful. Just be sure to get permission from that student. Providing detailed instructions and an example goes a long way in ensuring students know the expectations of a given assignment. Additionally, provide rubrics for all assignments, including discussions. If students know how they will be evaluated, they are more likely to complete the work properly. Furthermore, rubrics will minimize questions concerning point deductions and grades earned.

4. **Utilize differentiated instruction.** All students learn differently, and students in an online classroom are no exception. Provide students with multiple opportunities and formats for learning, including videos, audio lectures, and project choices that help engage and encourage learning for all students and preferences. Differentiated instruction promotes learning for all students, while also encouraging engagement in the online classroom.

5. **Encourage peer support and engagement.** Encourage students to communicate with their peers. Peer communication allows students to develop a network of support, rather than having students rely solely on the instructor. Allow students an opportunity to get to know one another in an introductory thread, and encourage students to connect throughout the course. Online learning can be lonely, but it does not have to be. Students can learn to develop a community in the online classroom.

Reprinted from *Faculty Focus*, July 15, 2016.

Wallflowers in the Online Classroom

by Jennifer Patterson Lorenzetti, editor of Academic Leader

What does it mean to be a wallflower? Such a person might be thought of as shy and might sit apart from others at a party or social gathering, choosing to listen and observe rather than participate. In the online classroom, a wallflower might be the person who reads course information and discussion boards regularly, but never posts. So how do instructors know if this online wallflower is really engaged in the course?

Angelique Hamane of Pepperdine University knows something about being a wallflower. "I learn from the periphery," she says, noting that she knows all about popular restaurants from perusing Yelp, and that she's a "virtual doctor" thanks to regular surfing of WebMD. She contends that this practice is typical. In a conference presentation, she advanced the idea that "in our everyday lives, we are engaged in learning without actually contributing." Why should the online classroom be any different?

A great deal of research supports the understanding that student engagement is linked to student success. Hamane defines engagement as "the amount of time and effort a student puts forth in academically purposeful activities." This time and effort is generally indicative of how well a student will learn and perform in the class. It is easy to assume that the more one posts, the more engaged one is.

In a face-to-face class, it is relatively easy to tell if students are engaged, even if they aren't continually contributing to class discussions. Students who appear awake, alert, and involved with the material (by taking notes, referencing textbooks, or giving the "a-ha" reaction to statements made in class) are generally engaged. On the other hand, students who are dozing, surfing the web, working on other assignments, or texting are probably not engaged with the material.

Online, however, it is not as easy to tell if a student is engaged with the material. Students either post or don't post to a discussion board, for example, and it is easy to assume that the more one posts, the more engaged one is.

Hamane and Pepperdine professor Farzin Madjidi set out to explore the issues surrounding student engagement in online classes. They posed two research questions:

- What is the relationship between student success and students' actual level of engagement as measured by an LMS?
- What is the relationship between student success and students' perceived level of engagement?

The study looked at students' final percentage scores in their online courses; actual levels of engagement as defined by frequency of forum views, posts, and replies; and perceived levels of engagement. Their results demonstrate that student engagement can take many forms, and student success can be linked to many types of engagement.

Study results and implications

The researchers first examined data on log-ons, simply measuring whether or not students logged into the LMS. Not surprisingly, "log-on had no correlation with student success," Hamane says. Just as a student in a face-to-face class needs to do more than simply walk through the classroom door, a student studying online needs to do more than just log on to the LMS.

The study also looked at which pages a student visited, and student visits to discussion boards correlated with student success. However, the students didn't have to post—they just needed to spend time there.

This simple finding leads to important implications for instructors and administrators who work with online courses. For example, Hamane encourages all students to visit and spend time on the discussion boards by writing exam questions that send the students back to the discussions to find information and craft their answers. She also posts "higher-order discussion questions" on the boards that require more than a yes/no answer, asking students to think and write more.

Hamane uses these findings to help students who may be struggling in class. "If students say they are having a hard time, I immediately look at reports to see who logs in" to discussions, she says. However, this can be a cumbersome process, so she suggests that administrators assist.

"Administrators can provide a support system. Extracting data can be time-consuming, so hire a programmer to [create] a dashboard" that allows instructors real-time information on student log-ins and activity online, suggests Hamane. The real-time data will be more valuable than that gathered after the course is completed.

Overall, it is important for administrators and instructors to understand that some "wallflower" students may be quite engaged in an online course without a lot of visible activity online. "Anecdotally, these students said they didn't like to put themselves out there," Hamane says.

Hamane notes that the presence of "wallflowers" in a course doesn't mean an instructor should avoid requirements for participation in discussion boards any more than a face-to-face instructor would not require a minimum amount of in-class discussion. Hamane still requires her online students to do a certain amount of posting, but she uses this requirement as a way for students to "scaffold" their skills and abilities to prepare for the next class. "I want them to post and write, but I understand it may not be in them," she says. "I understand when they don't [post]." This understanding is the biggest takeaway from the study. "There are students who are actually engaged, but we can't see it," Hamane says.

Reprinted from "The Perks of Being a Wallflower," *Distance Education Report* 18, no. 12 (2014): 1–2.

CHAPTER 4

•

Strategies for Student Engagement

How to Foster Critical Thinking and Student Engagement in Online Discussions

by Rob Kelly

Threaded discussions can provide excellent opportunities for students to engage in critical thinking. But critical thinking isn't an automatic feature of these discussions. It needs to be nurtured through clear expectations, carefully crafted questions, timely and useful feedback, and creative facilitation.

In an interview with *Online Classroom*, Texas Tech University instructors Marcus Tanner, Jillian Yarbrough, and Andrea McCourt discussed some of the principles of designing and managing threaded discussions that have helped their students engage with the material and each other in productive discussions.

Crafting questions

Discussion prompts play an essential role in soliciting meaningful discussion. Although there are opportunities for the instructor to spontaneously engage in asking questions, it's important to carefully plan and construct questions that progress from basic to advanced.

"I usually start my semester at the very basic level, asking knowledge questions, because I want everyone to get really comfortable in the discussion and feel that it's a safe place to share opinions and ideas," says McCourt, program director of Human Resource Development at Texas Tech. "If you're going to move up to synthesis or application, I think that takes several weeks of students taking chances and being rewarded in discussions, as well as giving them very well-written questions."

In addition to helping students become more comfortable in the online setting, lower-level questions can help them become more comfortable with the content. "Some of our students are not only learning to navigate, but this also might be a new topic to them, so it's difficult to jump immediately into synthesis or application," says Yarbrough, who teaches in the Human Resource Development program.

Lower-level questions need not be simple yes/no questions. For example, if the content describes a four-step process, rather than getting students to simply restate those steps, you can have them select which step is their favorite or state which they think is the most important and why. This provides the "lower-level regurgitation, and you can extend the question a little bit to have students talk about their preferences," McCourt says. "You can push it a little further."

Tanner, program director for Integrative Studies, adds, "It's not a yes/no question. It's a multipart question where in the first part, they're answering something at the low level, but the second part is midlevel. Even with the same discussion question, they're utilizing more than one level of Bloom's Taxonomy, so we're constantly challenging them to move higher."

Set expectations

Students need to know what is expected of them in threaded discussions. Describe expectations, provide a rubric, and demonstrate in the introductory discussion what you consider to be a substantive post.

"We have created our own rubrics. I apply them across the courses I teach, but each is going to have a slight modification from course to course because the discussion might have a different point value or a different emphasis. Sometimes the amount of participation required varies slightly from course to course," Yarbrough says.

The discussion board has the potential to bring together diverse perspectives. The key is to help students feel comfortable sharing. "We all have had different careers and different experiences. Embrace that, and say periodically, 'Share your perspective. Share your experiences. We're looking for you to share your unique ideas and experiences. It's important to be on topic, but there's no right or wrong answer,'" Yarbrough says.

That said, a substantive post needs to be more than just one's opinion. "Even though we may ask for their personal opinion about something, we're also expecting that opinion to come out of the course content. So when I'm grading those discussion board posts, I might write, 'This is a great thought that you had, but how is this connected to the course content for the week? What can you pull from the text or one of the lectures that would help substantiate what you're saying here?'" Tanner notes.

When McCourt asks students to include their opinions, she phrases the prompt carefully to say things such as, "Using your related life experiences, professional opinions, and information from the textbook, tell me…" This helps clarify the expectation that "it's not merely an opinion question," she says.

For students to get the highest grade on a post, McCourt requires them to cite outside resources—the textbook, a journal article, or a reputable website. "Even if I have a very opinion-heavy question, for full credit they know they have to cite something else," she says.

Students get graded on the discussions and see the rubric on a regular basis, but sometimes general feedback to all the students can help raise the level of the discussion. "I teach all undergraduate classes, and the trickiest thing for me to do is to get them to cite outside sources and do it well. When I provide the [discussion] model in the first week of the semester or so, I will actually give them a post where I cite a source and give an opinion. Sometimes, after I've graded the first week, I'll call their attention to the fact that the biggest problem I usually see in student responses is that they haven't cited outside resources. In my class feedback after the first week of the semester, I will frequently say, 'Here's the biggest area of omission. Look at my response to the discussion question. That's what I expect from you,'" McCourt says.

Managing participation

In addition to setting expectations and asking questions that will generate lively discussion, the instructor needs to monitor and facilitate the discussion to keep it on track and maximize learning.

At the beginning of each discussion, Tanner posts a "primer, providing a little bit more feedback in terms of what I'm looking for in an answer, and I might even provide a bit of an answer to the question as I see it."

At the end of the discussion, after he has graded it, Tanner posts a reflection. "I'll say, 'This is what I saw in terms of students' participation in this discussion. These are some really great points that were made.' Then I might also bring up some points that weren't made and even do some housekeeping things in those reflections, saying, 'You guys really need to stick close to the course content' or 'Make sure you're using APA style.'"

Yarbrough also provides a summary post, making sure that students see how each week's discussion builds on the previous week's. In addition, she might ask an additional question if she sees participation dwindling.

"I have the main discussion question, and of course I'm responding to students. But I can also post a new question that is related, and sometimes in these new questions, I might say something like 'Last week we talked about X, and now we're talking about Y. Let's discuss how X and Y are related,'" Yarbrough says.

The additional question is optional, but the idea is to generate new ideas and help students see how the content builds throughout the course.

When McCourt sees discussion decreasing, she rephrases the question or incorporates a current event or YouTube clip to get the conversation going again.

"I view my role as that of a moderator. I think if you establish yourself as an authority, you can shut down the discussion. So I make it a point in my syllabus and in the discussion that we're learning together. And when I respond to students, a lot of times I tell them, 'I will be playing the devil's advocate role, so I will question what you're saying. It's not because what you're saying is wrong. It's because I want to hear more ideas,'" McCourt says.

In addition, sometimes students need to be redirected in the discussion board. "If I get a response that I need to send in a different direction or correct a little bit, I always try to find something in that student's response that is positive. 'I really liked your unique approach and the way you did this. That's the first time I've seen it described that way. Have you thought about this…?' I try to very gently redirect as a moderator, because I think discussion needs to be fostered, and I do think an instructor can shut it down. Also, I would never tell a student in a public forum, 'You're wrong,'" McCourt notes.

Feedback

Rubrics help streamline the grading process, but sometimes it's important to provide additional feedback to students that the other students don't see. This feedback might be a simple compliment on a good post, or it might be more in-depth coaching.

"I usually save my qualitative feedback for students who have gone above and beyond expectations or when I need to provide additional feedback for students who are struggling," McCourt says. "I do not respond to every student each week. I try to keep a running tally of who I responded to each week, so I interact with everyone throughout the semester in the public forum. I try to interact equally with all students in discussion boards rather than responding just to early posters."

Reprinted from *Online Classroom*, August 2014.

Five Ways to Foster Creativity in Your Online Classroom

by Oliver Dreon, Millersville University

When I talk to instructors who are new to teaching online, many complain about the sterile nature of their online courses. While they interact with their students and support their learning, they often miss some of the creativity that students bring to a face-to-face classroom. In face-to-face environments, they argue, students can more easily demonstrate their creativity by participating in role-playing, leading class discussions, or giving presentations, for example. These instructors see the online classroom as a different space. Because most of the interactions in the online realm are text-based, the instructors don't always see the same creativity on display. In their online classes, instructors will assign readings and have their students post to discussion boards. Instructors may also lead synchronous lessons to help students learn concepts. At the end of the module, the instructors will assess learning by having students submit papers to the course dropbox or take an online exam. After completing one module, the instructor and students progress to the next module, where this cycle of instruction, interaction, and assessment is often repeated. Employing such a repetitious learning cycle, it's no wonder that my colleagues who are new to online teaching don't see the vibrancy of the online classroom.

The reality, however, is that the online classroom can be a space that supports and showcases student creativity. The learning management system can become a place where students expand their learning beyond traditional online means. With a host of free tools available on the Internet, online students have the ability to demonstrate their creative side as part of the class's interactions and assessments. Wondering where to get started? Here are a few suggestions to help you be successful.

1. **View your classroom as a commons area.** Some online instructors see the content section of their course as the most valuable component of instruction. While it's important for students to have easy access to quality course materials and learning objects, the communication areas of an online course are where students will feel the most supported. In these sections, the instructor can interact with students and build a social presence that fosters learning. Threaded discussions are critical places for students to demonstrate their understanding of course content and to collectively make meaning of the subject matter. But online communication tools can do more than just foster discourse. Students can also use these spaces to share their creative works. For instance, as an introductory activity in my online class, I have students use an online tool such as MyBrainShark or Animoto to create short videos in order to introduce themselves to their classmates. The videos are shared in a discussion board and inevitably spark conversations. I also use the assignment as a pre-test where I ask students to share what they know about the course. Used in this manner, the discussion board becomes a virtual gallery where students get to "see" their classmates and also get to showcase their creativity.

2. **Leave your assignments open-ended.** While it's important to explicitly outline your expectations for students, consider leaving the actual mode of expression more open-ended. Is it important that students write a five-page paper to demonstrate they've learned a topic? Could they create a video outlining their understanding instead? Could they use the course content to animate an academic discussion on the topic? Providing students with options will increase their buy-in for an assignment and allow them to show more of their creative talents. It's also good pedagogically. The National Center on Universal Design for Learning (*www.udlcenter.org*) recommends giving students multiple means of expression and action in classroom environments. While UDL principles have traditionally been applied to face-to-face classrooms, the concepts are equally relevant to online spaces.

3. **Think about creativity differently.** While some people view creativity as an elusive construct that is hard to define, there's actually a body of research that helps bring clarity to the concept. J. P. Guilford (1977) identified four characteristics of creative thinking: fluency, flexibility, elaboration, and originality. *Fluency* describes a person's ability to generate a large number of ideas, solutions, or responses. *Flexibility* examines someone's ability to look at a situation

from a different point of view. *Elaboration* encompasses a person's ability to modify or expand an existing idea. *Originality*, often seen as the essence of creativity, is the ability to generate a unique idea, product, or solution. While Guilford's framework helps describe the concept of creativity in much more operational terms, the model also provides opportunities for the online classroom. Instead of giving an online quiz on a topic, why not have students see the content from a different point? A chemistry instructor could have students explain an oxidation reaction from the point of view of an electron, for instance. A history instructor could choose to focus on the elaboration aspects of creativity and have students outline a debate that argues both sides of a controversial topic. With an animation application such as GoAnimate (*goanimate.com*), the students could demonstrate their understanding of the course concepts and while showcasing their creativity.

4. **View assessments more broadly.** In the online classroom, instructors sometimes focus too heavily on objective assessments such as quizzes and exams. While these are relatively easy to design, schedule, and grade, such assessments offer few opportunities for students' creative expression. By expanding the assessments to include student-produced videos, presentations, animations, and artistic works, instructors can foster student creativity while evaluating student understanding.

5. **Don't be distracted by the shiny.** One challenge with using online creative tools for assessments and interaction in online classrooms is the influence student-produced media can have on instructors' evaluation of classroom learning. While a video created by a student may look appealing or technically challenging, the learning demonstrated through the work may be sparse. Don't let a highly polished project influence your assessment of student learning. In some cases, it may be beneficial to include a rubric that clearly identifies aspects of the assignment that will be assessed. This can help focus students on the specific content they need to demonstrate in their creative work.

While traditional use of the online classroom offers a variety of means of instruction, interaction, and assessment, seeing the space as an environment where students can display their creativity can help build student interest and engage them more in the learning process. It can also help the online classroom evolve into a more vibrant, creative space.

Reprinted from *Online Classroom*, January 2014.

Ten Ways to Motivate and Engage Your Online Learners

by Rob Kelly

Motivation and engagement play a central role in student success and satisfaction. However, the online learning environment poses special challenges. Without proper course design and facilitation, it's all too easy for online learners to feel isolated, bored, and unengaged with the materials. Here, Paul Beaudoin, assistant humanities professor at Fitchburg State University, discusses motivation and engagement strategies he has found to be effective in the award-winning online courses he teaches.

Instructor participation

"If you do only one thing, participate in your classes," Beaudoin advises. "Make sure your students know you're there in the course with them by participating with them in their learning."

Effective instructor participation includes responding promptly to students' questions or emails. "When students email me, it's like raising their hand in class. They want to be noticed as soon as possible. I make sure that even if I can't immediately answer their email, I can let them know that I've read it and will get back to them within 24 hours," Beaudoin says. "An effective instructor will acknowledge when learners are doing well and not so well. An email applauding an excellent grade by one or a message to another who may not be achieving as much as he or she should" will go a long way toward personalizing the online learning environment.

Beaudoin suggests reading as many discussion board posts as you can and responding to them in a timely manner. "When students know you are actively participating, they are more likely to take responsibility for how they contribute to the online class. When I reply, I always start with the name of the student and then follow through with a comment that directly reflects the student's post. For example, I might write 'Rhonda, I read your post today on X and I don't agree with…' or 'Elaine, your post on Y was well thought out and organized, and you articulated a really important point…' These kinds of posts change the dynamic I have with my learners, and they stand as examples of good responses in a discussion board. It will encourage your learners to think more reflectively about what they will post. Isn't that a win-win?"

How-to video

For many students, the online learning environment may be completely new. To help orient students to the design and expectations of his courses, Beaudoin includes a 12-minute video tutorial that explains the course's layout and function. After the video, students take a short quiz to check that they have viewed the video and understand what to expect in the course.

Vary the learning experience

A course that follows the same pattern—read this chapter, answer these questions—module after module can be a major motivation killer. "Students always know what to expect. They can actually come to dread it as much as one would dread a monotone lecture," Beaudoin says. "I try to create learning modules that encompass all kinds of learning materials—readings, lectures, activities, games. I mix it up so that students don't become uninterested."

Course map

Although Beaudoin likes to vary the learning experience, he designs his courses so that the module content is arranged in a clear and logical order. He then creates a course map to help students navigate. The course map is a downloadable PDF document that provides a complete list of elements within each module. It outlines how long each lecture is, what the learning objective for that module is, whether there are readings or additional media, what the discussion board topic will be, and whether the module contains activities or a quiz. Students are given an area to check off the materials they have completed for each module, allowing them to visualize the progress they are making through the course.

Icebreakers

Like many instructors, Beaudoin uses icebreakers to encourage students to connect with each other by sharing their interests, major, year in school, etc. In addition, he has students visit each other's pages within Blackboard and post messages to make connections. Because he teaches music and art classes, he has created the "Museum of Me" icebreaker, in which students create a "museum" of the things that are important to them in their own lives, be it family, friends, hobbies, work, education, etc. Students are required to visit at least three other museums with the hope of finding others in the class with similar interests—but most students visit all their peers' museums. "Not only am I introducing them to the concept of the class [an appreciation for the art and music of years past] but I'm getting them to think about their own lives and those of their colleagues. The kinds of bonds that are made between the learners in my class are genuine and often continue well past the end of the semester. That bond helps students feel less isolated and more responsible for the kinds of learning taking place in the online environment."

Incentives

To help learners meet goals and deadlines, Beaudoin creates incentives that motivate them. For example, he creates a checklist for the materials that students need to complete before midterm. "If they are able to check off all the items on the list by a specific deadline, I'll give them an extra 10 points. It's a feel-good, positive reinforcement measure. The extra 10 points don't really change their grades, but it gets them thinking 'I can get 10 extra points if I can do this by this particular time,' and that motivates them," Beaudoin says.

Games

Activities such as digital scavenger hunts, crossword puzzles, and word searches can engage students. "I want my students to realize the devices they use to connect to the Internet are really powerful. I'll divide my class into smaller groups and have them do scavenger hunts to find materials they are actually going to be working with later in the course. The winning group gets bonus points and recognition on the course home page," Beaudoin says. Meanwhile, word searches and crossword puzzles help learners memorize new vocabulary or important concepts. Students are given bonus points when they complete the activities successfully.

With the permission of the winning group, Beaudoin creates a "Wall of Achievement" on the course announcements page, listing the students who have achieved the most success with any incentive. He has noticed that "learners will work very hard to get their names on that wall, and that kind of 'public' recognition goes a long way toward creating and sustaining motivation and engagement."

Surveys

Halfway through his courses, Beaudoin creates an anonymous survey, asking students to provide feedback (e.g., "The professor is responsive to my emails"), prompting self-reflection (e.g., "I want to learn more about…"), and including "just for fun" social questions (e.g., "If you could have dinner with a famous person, who would it be, and why?"). The survey is his opportunity to adjust the course and address the needs of the learners. "Each course is a unique group of learners with different experiences, learning backgrounds, and abilities. The midpoint survey allows me to take an anonymous picture of that group and adjust my strategies as necessary," he reports. "And don't be surprised when your learners are honest and forthcoming about what is and isn't working right for them."

Newsletters

"I can send my learners an email, but graphically it isn't engaging, and they're likely not going to read (or pay attention) to the whole thing," Beaudoin notes. He was inspired to change his strategy when he received one of those "family Christmas newsletters" that despite all his misgivings, he was compelled to read all the way through. "I realized I could harness that by creating a newsletter for my class."

Beaudoin creates and sends out newsletters twice in each of his online courses—at midterm and just before the final. By using graphics and humor to convey information that is important at these times, he greatly improves the effectiveness of the message. For example, a two-page newsletter before the final features a photo of a worried-looking young man holding a sign that reads "The end is near," a calendar with a circled date indicating the final due date, an announcement for the end-of-course survey, an invitation to check grades, and a news item that relates to the course content. The newsletter will always include Beaudoin's email contact information as well, reminding students yet again that he is always available to them.

Relevance

Beaudoin makes it a point to demonstrate how the course material relates to students' lives, professions, and educational goals. This is particularly important when students are taking the course because it's a requirement and not necessarily something they would personally be interested in taking.

Introducing concepts by using examples students can relate to is a great way to engage them. "Imagine your favorite sports team is having a winning streak. Just how probable is it that the winning streak will continue? That's a great way for a statistics class to begin. Or imagine that the best baseball batting average at the moment is about a .350. I ask my students how they would feel if their favorite musician hit only 35 percent of the notes. By connecting the course material to current events, I take a subject that learners might not be very interested in and get them thinking about it. If I can find a way to create relevancy to students' lives, I can open a door to a new world, even if just a crack," Beaudoin says.

He admits that "it's an exciting time to be in education—the world is open and anyone can learn anything, anyplace, anytime." However, that sea of openness can be a challenge for the student sitting in front of the computer feeling there is nowhere to turn. These 10 tips for motivating and engaging your online learners are a starting place for you to think about the kinds of needs your learners have and an encouragement to think creatively about addressing them.

Reprinted from *Online Classroom,* February 2014.

Online Learning That Lasts: Three Ways to Increase Student Engagement and Retention

by Tyler Griffin, Brigham Young University

It is not uncommon for students in online courses to experience one or more of the following frustrations:

- "I don't love the subject, but I have to take this class to graduate."
- "I'm not invested in this class because I don't feel connected with the material, the teacher, or other students."
- "I rarely learn anything in this class that I will remember or use after the term ends."
- "I am losing motivation to complete assignments or turn in my work on time."

All these issues can lead to a much larger concern: students who finally conclude, "I don't care about this class anymore. I'm dropping out."

It is easy to assume that these problems are mostly due to the subject matter. While we can't necessarily change *what* needs to be taught, we can always change *how* we package it. And ironically, when we make the right adjustments, we will find improvement in all the trouble areas listed above. So, what can we do to facilitate meaningful experiences that lead to higher levels of student satisfaction and long-term learning that lasts far beyond the end of the course?

Begin by realizing that you most likely don't need a complete course redesign to engage and retain more students at higher levels. You can start by making simple yet strategic changes that immediately improve student engagement and learning in the courses you already teach. You just need to know what to do and where to start.

Here are three techniques you can use in your courses that will improve learning and retention in your online classes: (1) front-load the relevance, (2) maximize the strengths of online learning tools without migrating face-to-face teaching weaknesses and constraints to digital classes, and (3) help students learn at more than one or two levels of cognitive engagement.

Front-loaded relevance

Too often, teachers wait until the *end* of a course, a unit, or a class session to "pull back the curtain" and reveal the big moment of connection for everything they've taught, only to be disappointed when the students seem completely unimpressed and unmoved. By giving the students just enough relevant context at the beginning of a course or a lesson, we give them a reason to stay focused on what we are about to teach without them "zoning out." The intent of front-loaded relevance is to create a "cognitive vacuum" in the students. This serves to activate their curiosity, pique their interest, or trigger an innate desire to resolve problems or gain a sense of understanding.

Initial relevance building should take only a few minutes. In practice, this can be accomplished by using a concise and applicable problem, short story, video clip, or case study, followed by a prompt such as, "Now, let's explore a few theories/concepts/processes/practices or products that could help you make sense of this situation or solve this problem." Returning to the initial problem or scenario at the end of class will help students recognize that they are learning and see meaningful connections between your course and their lives outside school.

There are many less complicated ways to increase relevance at the beginning of class. Consider how you could implement some of the following techniques before presenting new material:

- Poll students on their level of confidence in a widely held belief that relates to your lesson. This will get them thinking about the material at deeper levels, and they will more likely stay engaged to find a resolution.
- Show students a picture of an object that could be metaphorically related to your topic and ask them to make connections between the object and the topic. Their understanding of the tangible object will help inform their lack of understanding of the abstract subject. When helpful, keep referring them back to the object at different points of the online lesson.

- Take whatever synthesis question you were going to ask at the end of your class and ask it at the beginning. This helps the students see where you are trying to take them. This is similar to showing a person the picture on a puzzle box before they try to put any pieces together.
- Use a relevant "Look for…" or "Watch for…" statement before having students read a block of text, watch a movie, perform an experiment, or work on an assignment. This will increase student focus and engagement and decrease their feelings of disconnectedness with the material.

Front-loaded relevance is effective only to the degree that teachers use examples, scenarios, questions, or objects that are truly applicable to students outside class. While preparing for a class, ask yourself, "Whose questions am I trying to help the students answer—mine or theirs?" The more we focus on students' needs, the more engaged the students will be and the more they will keep performing at higher levels for us.

Maximize online learning strengths, minimize face-to-face weaknesses

Online teachers often migrate face-to-face techniques and paradigms to their digital classes. While many principles and practices of effective teaching work well in both settings, it is important to recognize that each has strengths and weaknesses and to adjust accordingly.

One of the major strengths of online learning is its ability to maintain high levels of ongoing engagement through responsibility from the learners. In many traditional classroom settings, students can easily disengage from the flow of class and still receive points for being present. They feel comfortable letting their minds wander, knowing that the highly motivated students in the room will answer all of the instructor's discussion questions. They also know they can "cram" for tests and get help on assignments from others when needed.

Online students can slip into passive learning mode more easily than can traditional classroom students, who are surrounded by others who can see their outward behaviors. Knowing this, online teachers should implement frequent opportunities for *all* students to respond to simple learning checks and be accountable for what is being covered. If credit for a day's class is based on reasonably spaced, short measurements of competency or on student reflections, students will quickly learn to stay focused and engaged. This will prevent them from having to spend extra time backtracking to find answers or missed information before they can proceed with the next part of the lesson.

To implement this principle, find natural breaks in each day's lesson and insert a short quiz, a discussion board requirement, or other response form. Carefully monitor student responses to adjust for an ideal range of difficulty and complexity for these mastery checks. If the questions or tasks are too difficult or complex, student frustration will increase and class engagement and retention will actually decrease. If they are too simple, students will disengage more often, knowing they will be able to pass your competency checks without paying attention to the material along the way. Depending on your students, you may also find that it helps to attach a low point value to some or all of these checkpoints for increased motivation to stay focused.

Use many levels of learning

Educational taxonomies are a way of classifying various orders of learning processes. Bloom's Taxonomy has been the most widely used since 1956, when it was first published. It consists of six layers (in increasing order of complexity): remember, understand, apply, analyze, evaluate, and create. Online classes that expect students to learn and perform at all six layers are more likely to engage and retain students than those that focus only on one or two.

Since testing what students remember or understand is usually easier than assessing something they create or evaluate, many faculty traditionally put more focus in their courses on the two lower levels of Bloom's Taxonomy. Online instructors should analyze their courses to find where more complex learning objectives could reasonably be integrated to activate different levels of learning in their students.

With imagination, a teacher can include application, analysis, evaluation, and creation levels of learning on tests. These levels of learning are more naturally integrated, however, in small-group work settings, individual assignments, term-long projects, or learning portfolios. Online courses naturally allow students to connect with other class members across space and time to work together on these higher-order objectives. With the proliferation and mastery of technology tools today, our students are also well equipped to create projects, presentations, portfolios, and apps.

Students cannot learn at the higher levels of the taxonomy without fully employing the lower levels of remembering and understanding. However, students who create something meaningful for your class are far more likely to remember and understand what they learned than those who are just asked to memorize and understand critical facts and details about your field of study.

Conclusion

When integrating new strategies into your online courses, remember to pace yourself. Don't try to change everything all at once or you will likely become overwhelmed and fail. Pick a few of your favorite suggestions and try implementing them. Once they are working naturally for you, try experimenting with others.

Your students are perhaps your greatest asset in making course improvements. Be open and honest with them about your desires and efforts to make your class more meaningful and engaging. Let them know of your concern regarding their successful completion of your class. Occasionally ask them for feedback as you experiment with new techniques or course designs, and be open to their suggestions. They will appreciate the fact that you are focused on improving the learning experience for them as students.

Reprinted from *Online Classroom*, July 2014.

Ensuring Student Success in Online Courses

by Poonam Kumar and Marilyn Skrocki, Saginaw Valley State University

Students like online classes due to their flexibility and convenience. But not all students do well in these courses; statistics indicate that online classes have a much higher dropout rate compared to traditional face-to-face classes. The attrition rates in online courses tend to be 10 to 20 percent higher than in face-to-face classes. While certain personal factors that could influence a student's decision to drop out, many of the factors are related to institutional and course level support—and these barriers can be addressed with thoughtful planning and implementation. Institutional-level factors like technical support, academic support, advising, and availability of resources can support student success in online courses. At the course level, there are many simple strategies and techniques that instructors can use to support students' success in their online classes.

Course organization and layout

Many students drop out of online courses because they feel overwhelmed and sometimes frustrated with the amount of information presented to them and the way it is presented. Learners can experience "cognitive overload" if the information presented to them is not logically organized and the course design is not easy to follow. In such cases, learners will end up spending a lot of mental energy just trying to figure out how the course is organized and how to find information, and may end up feeling overwhelmed and frustrated. Thoughtful course design and layout can minimize this frustration and help students focus on the content rather than on navigation issues.

- Provide a simple and consistent layout and navigation for the course. Use the same layout for each module (for example, overview, objectives, readings, viewings, assignments, etc.; differentiate between required and recommended reading), as too much variation could overwhelm students.

- For variety, present some information via the visual channel and some information via the verbal channel.
- Explain and show the structure and layout of the course by making a "course tour" video.

Clearly communicate expectations

Many students report feeling lost and confused in online learning environments. Due to lack of face-to-face contact, students are sometimes unclear on the instructor's expectations or need reassurance that they understand those expectations.

- Provide detailed and very explicit instructions about the course format, assignments, expectations, grading criteria, etc.
- Provide a "Frequently Asked Questions" section with a list of questions that students may have about the course.
- Provide rubrics and sample assignments. Creating a short video tutorial explaining the rubric and assignment gives students a very concrete idea of the expectations.
- Consider employing a quiz tool to ensure students comprehend their course responsibilities as outlined in the syllabus. With this technique, students are allowed multiple attempts to take the quiz under low pressure, which ensures confidence when utilizing the LMS quiz tool function.

Prepare students

Many times, students enroll in online courses without a realistic understanding of what it takes to be a successful learner in an online environment. Online learning environments are better suited for students who are self-disciplined, motivated, and know how to manage their time. An orientation to online learning and tips on how to succeed in online courses can better prepare all students for online courses.

The student orientation should include discussions of:
- Technical skills
- Understanding of online/hybrid learning environments
- Study skills
- Workload management
- Communication
- Resources, including technical help and other campus resources

- Personal introductory video of the instructor in a nonacademic light
- A library of resources on issues affecting online instruction, such as time management, computer accessibility, willingness to reach out with questions, etc.

Chunk the content and scaffold instruction

Sometimes the workload and reading requirements in online courses may seem daunting to students, especially if they don't have very good time management and prioritization skills. Chunking and organizing the content meaningfully into modules/units not only makes it easy for students to understand and remember the concepts but also makes it more manageable for them. By doing this, the instructor can present complex concepts or ideas as "bite-size information" so students can understand, apply, and retain that information. By incorporating assessments and feedback with every learning module, instructors have the opportunity to scaffold students' learning.

- Divide big assignments or projects into smaller milestones to help students manage the workload, and provide feedback at each step.
- Provide review sessions or instructional videos where you notice gaps in learning to clarify concepts.

Humanize the course

Students report that one of the main reasons they drop out of online courses or programs is because they feel lonely and isolated. Learning is a social activity; we learn through interactions and discussions with others. In the absence of face-to-face contact, online learning can be an isolating experience if there are no opportunities to interact with others in the course. Humanize the online experience through personal interactions and stories and add the human touch to it.

- Set a warm, welcoming tone right in the beginning of the course to connect with students.
- Do ice-breaking activities to create a community of learners; ask students to share personal profiles, bios, stories, and other examples of personal information.
- Offer a "live" orientation session through Skype or any other online conferencing tool so students have the opportunity to interact with you in real time.
- Provide a discussion forum for non-course-related social interactions.
- Encourage peer-to-peer support.
- Incorporate group work.
- Interact with students by providing a personal response on their

personal profile.
- Encourage students to contact you when commenting on their assignments or discussion postings; a simple "as always, contact me with any questions" note helps make students more comfortable seeking additional information.

These simple strategies will help students succeed in your courses.

Reprinted from *Online Classroom,* June 2015.

Gamifying an Online Course: It's Not a Class, It's a Story

by Robert Prince, University of Alaska Fairbanks

A few years ago, I was struck by a question: What makes students so mo-tivated to engage in "work" doing tasks in video games, yet at the same time so regularly unmotivated to do work in class that could actually benefit them and their careers? That's when I discovered the concept of gamifica-tion—the process of applying the motivational techniques used in video games to courses. What are video games doing so right that I wasn't doing in my classes? It turned out to be quite a few things. I decided to try imple-menting games as part of a major revision to my Journalism 101: Media & Culture online course with the help of instructional designers Owen Guth-rie, Jennifer Moss, and Dan LaSota from the University of Alaska Fairbanks E-Learning department.

Story

A great video game has a story behind it, one that is engaging and makes you sympathize with the characters. So what kind of story can you create about a Media & Culture course designed to educate students on the mass media and build their media literacy skills? Well, for a good story we need conflict. We need protagonists fighting for a good cause and antago-nists trying to stop them. In the world of journalism today, one of the most pervasive conflicts involves newspapers struggling to survive. Many papers have been absorbed by larger corporations more interested in turning profits than in turning out solid reporting. So I decided the story behind the class would be that my students were interns at a newspaper that was struggling to stay privately owned rather than go public and have to start answering to stockholders. I created an elaborate history behind the family that owned the paper in an effort to make the students sympathize with the characters and want to save the paper. How would they save the paper? By collectively gathering enough "views" to save it. In other words, if they all did well on their homework, the paper would be saved.

Points

One of the more amusing revelations I had in this process was related to how I handled points in my classes. In a normal class, my students start out with an "A" the first day of class, and that grade goes down if any of their assignments are below A-level work. It's the complete opposite in video games. I've never seen a game in which you start out essentially having won the game and the more you play, the more you lose. You always start a video game with zero points, and you're motivated to play more so you can build that number up higher and higher to impress your friends and/or gain skills or other perks. So I started the students at zero points and referred to points as views. If they did great work, more people would read it online, they'd get more views, and their grade would go up.

Website

A successful video game creates what we call a "suspension of disbelief" within its players. This means that the story is convincing enough that the player feels it could be true. It was important to me that the class website look like a real online portal for a newspaper, or the students would not buy the backstory at all. So we came up with a Wordpress design that was fairly convincing. I wrote up some fake stories to populate the site, and the students' work would eventually fill it in with plenty of material. This worked well with one exception: We still had to rely on the Blackboard side of the course for quizzes, tests, and posting grades, and that crushed any hopes I had for suspending my students' disbelief. We made up an excuse for Blackboard, telling the students it was our "Human Resources" portal, but there was no covering it up. Until Blackboard is customizable like Wordpress or Wordpress is reasonably capable of doing the job of Blackboard, this element of the class will wreak havoc on my efforts to suspend disbelief.

Levels

Another characteristic of a great video game is that it allows you rise through levels as you play, gaining certain powers and abilities with each new level. One of the benefits of the newsroom story I was creating was that I could use the jobs in the paper as levels for the students. As they gained more points in the class by doing the coursework, they would level up and acquire titles like copy editor, news editor, and finally editor-in-chief. Each time they reached an established milestone of points, they'd get a letter from the newspaper's executive assistant congratulating them and explaining the benefits of their new position. One of the fun parts of putting this class together was trying to think of perks that would feel like real rewards to students but wouldn't always be just extra credit or getting out of work. Some of the perks we came up with were getting to choose your own group partners and submitting a story for the front page of the online paper. As a little experiment, I gave students who made the editor-in-chief level the opportunity to give out 1,000 points of extra credit (equivalent to 1 percent of their final grade) to any one of their classmates or to divide it up among several students. I was interested to see how knowing your classmate might eventually have extra credit points to hand out would affect group dynamics in the course.

Execution

This gamified class was a major revision of the original course, which was essentially an online correspondence course I had inherited from another faculty member. Students interact much more than they did before, and their assignments are much more interesting to read. I haven't yet tallied the official numbers, but I feel student success in completing the course has improved.

Creating your own gamified course

My first step was finding a conflict within my field to set as the basis for my class story. What are the conflicts in the field you're teaching? Next, consider the levels your students might progress through, and try to make them cool enough to be worth striving for. Finally, consider what rewards you can offer for achieving these levels. That can be a fun and creative process, and polling your current students for ideas isn't a bad start.

What I can tell you about gamifying a course is that you should do it for yourself, first and foremost. It's a great deal more work to come up with a story for your course and implement these nontraditional elements. But at the same time, it's a much more satisfying and interesting way to teach. When you try to change the status quo to teach more effectively, you can meet with ambivalence or straight-up resistance. In the end, however, this class represents me and my commitment to education, and I want it to reflect my desire to innovate and experiment rather than just tread down the same old well-worn path.

Reprinted from *Online Classroom*, June 2015.

The Impact of Instructor Posts on Student Participation: An Interview with Cheryl Murphy, University of Arkansas

Many online educators preach that instructors should be active in discussion, but not monopolize it, yet we do not have any real research that demonstrates how instructor involvement affects student participation in discussion. Cheryl Murphy, associate professor of educational technology at the University of Arkansas, has done research on this subject, and found that the quantity of instructor involvement did not affect the quality of student postings, but it was negatively correlated to the quantity of student postings. This suggests that instructor involvement can reach a point of diminishing returns. Here, Murphy discusses her findings and their implications for the online classroom.

Why might more instructor participation in discussion reduce student participation?
Learners may come to rely on the instructor to carry the discussion, leading students to take a more passive role. This would be similar to a face-to-face classroom environment where, as instructors, we can stymie good student discussion and lull students into passive learning roles simply by inserting ourselves into the conversation. But, as Conrad and Donaldson point out, because many students have been educated in a predominately lecture-based environment, they may actually be more comfortable taking a passive online role.

We also found that when students received no instructor intervention, they posted more frequently. One possible explanation is that the group who received no instructor guidance may have felt the need to work with peers to clarify understandings and share resources. Students may have been interacting more frequently to provide resources and support to each other in the absence of the instructor.

You also suggest that less instructor involvement might have led students to package their posts differently. How so?

Even when student participation is minimal, posts can be extremely focused and extensive, and can exhibit deep levels of understanding. Our findings indicated that students posted less often with instructor intervention, yet scored just as well on the quality measure as did students who did not receive instructor intervention. This could lead a reader to infer two things: that instructor intervention helped students create posts that were more focused, so that they were expressing the same quality of ideas in less time, or that the group members who received no instructor guidance may have been posting more frequently to provide clarification, resources, and support to each other in the absence of the instructor.

These two potential explanations mirror what can occur in an in-class group discussion activity. If the instructor provides a prompting question and follows up by suggesting resources and key points that groups should consider, versus providing a prompting question without additional guidance, we would expect the group discussions in the first scenario to be more focused than those in the second.

Is there agreement within the literature on what amount of instructor participation is ideal in an online course?

There are a wide range of thoughts on this topic, with researchers such as Andresen recommending as little instructor posting as possible, and others such as Bedi and Brookfield and Preskill arguing that instructors must maintain a substantive and ongoing posting presence. Personally, we take the middle ground and advocate for a balanced instructor intervention that offers guidance, but does not lead to overreliance.

Murphy's research leaves open the question of the "sweet spot" of instructor involvement in discussion. But it also raises more fundamental questions about the purpose of discussion that any online instructor should consider to guide his or her own participation in discussion. Does the instructor want to use participation to force student engagement with the course topics? In that case, quantity might be the most important goal.

Is discussion instead used to develop critical thinking skills, in which case quality might be more important? Murphy mentions that discussion participation can be used as a formative assessment to gauge class understanding and react to widespread misunderstandings. In this case, the instructor might be more interested in corralling discussion so that students can show they understand the material, rather than allowing it to run to different topics.

Despite efforts to flatten the hierarchy of an online course, anything that an instructor does is done as an authority, and thus can have chilling effects on student involvement. As online instructors, we think our involvement in discussion can only improve its quality, but that may not be the case. Maybe it just orients discussion toward the topics that interest us. Online instructors need to carefully consider the purpose of discussion and the effects their own involvement will have in it in order to gauge how much involvement is right for their courses.

Reference

Murphy, C., and R. Fortner. "Impact of Instructor Intervention on the Quality and Frequency of Student Discussion Posts in a Blended Classroom." *MERLOT Journal of Online Learning and Teaching* 10, no. 3 (2014): 337–50.

Reprinted from *Online Classroom,* August 2014.

Maximizing Engagement in the Flipped Classroom: An Interview with Ronald A. Yaros, Phillip Merrill College of Journalism

The flipped classroom (a technique also called "blended learning") has become a hot topic in education over the past few years. The concept makes perfect sense. Traditional courses are set up to "push" content out to students during a face-to-face meeting, and then requires them to apply that content to assignments done outside of class.

But in this model, the student who is having problems on an assignment does not have the instructor there to ask for help. The flipped classroom solves that problem by moving the content phase outside class, and the application phase to inside the classroom. The advent of easy video production and hosting means that there is no longer a reason for students to be at a certain place at a certain time to view a lecture. The lecture can be recorded and put online for them to view on their own. This frees up class time to work with materials that generate engagement with the content.

But many instructors have had a hard time finding activities that truly engage the students in class. Often they fall into the "lecturing and clicking" mentality of pushing content, but with periodic polls or surveys. While these activities are better than nothing, they are often not truly engaging. Look at the screens of your students' laptops during class, and you will most likely learn that much of their attention is devoted to other websites, email, or texting. This has led even faculty as forward-thinking and tech-savvy as Clay Shirky to ban electronic devices from his courses.

But Ronald Yaros, associate professor of journalism at the University of Maryland–College Park, has found both a technique and a technology to keep students' attention and maximize engagement in the flipped classroom. He first notes that laptops quickly produce "what Linda Stone calls 'continuous partial attention' between a presentation and their laptop. When given the option to either look at slides or view websites on a laptop, limited digital self-regulation quickly makes the laptop a distraction."

However, laptops are not the only option for in-class devices. Yaros has his students bring tablets to class. He then uses an app called "Nearpod" to host the class content and interactive strategies. Nearpod allows instructors to post a variety of different types of content on the app for students to view from their own tablets, from slides to websites, videos, and the like. It also provides a number of means to gather feedback and engage students, including polls, surveys, and discussion.

Here Yaros adds a twist. Instead of projecting his slides on a screen at the front of the room, which allows the class to put some other content on their own devices, he only projects the content to Nearpod. He runs whatever content he wants to use on his own tablet using Nearpod, which the students watch on their own tablets. Thus, "students no longer have the *option* to 'multitask,' or switch between projected slides and their laptops, which could lead to distraction. Now, if students aren't engaging and interacting with class content on their mobile device, they'll miss key concepts, explanations, class discussions, and my questions about the content that they produced."

Yaros goes on to say, "I use the Nearpod app to share the presentation via WiFi. The Nearpod app is free to students, without the need to create an online account. I easily convert my slides for display in Nearpod and conduct real-time polls (goodbye clickers), as well as ask open-ended questions for text responses that I can share anonymously on everyone's device. We can also view live Twitter feeds and PDF documents that I share with the class."

Yaros also sweetens the pot by having students use some of the outside-of-class time to generate inside-of-class content. Instead of just recording and posting traditional lectures for students to watch outside class, he makes use of Twitter and Blogger to have his students create content that will be discussed in class. As he says, "At the beginning of the semester, I distribute a semester-long schedule of five rotating teams for each chapter in the course. From day one, every student knows the team he or she is on during any given week and the deadline for posting content. After I introduce the chapter and summarize the key concepts, every student is expected to research, produce, and post his or her own course-related content before our next class meeting.

"The team assignments that detail specific content to post are announced that week. For example, students assigned to the rotating Twitter team research and post course-related tweets, which are displayed for all to read on our course blog (*http://150masscomm.blogspot.com*). A second team posts 150 words on the course blog, explaining their research of the chapter's topic. To manage my grading time, only students in a third team research, produce, and post comprehensive multimedia content for their own ePortfolio, which is listed on the right-hand column of the course blog. This means that I'm reading and grading the longest postings from only a small portion of the class. Students in a fourth team post summaries of the assigned readings, and the final team must review the postings of their peers to provide constructive feedback. All students use the time between classes to produce and post their content, which will be synthesized and discussed for the second component in my blended course, our face-to-face meetings."

Yaros reports, "The results and the student feedback have been amazing. My two-week experiment last fall compared the same content, taught by the same teacher (me) in the same room and on the same days to two sections of 60 undergraduates. One section used the Nearpod app on a tablet or phone. The other section viewed the traditional projected PowerPoint slides with no devices. Quiz results suggested no statistically significant differences between Nearpod and the traditional sections, but students' ratings of course enjoyment and relevance were significantly higher in the Nearpod section. It is important to note that most of the research to date reports that laptops reduce attention and learning, compared to classes without laptops. My results suggest that it's not the technology per se, but the type of devices used and *how* that technology is supported. In this case, devices did not reduce learning and, in fact, increased enjoyment of the class."

Yaros goes on to say, "Even classes that are totally online could use Nearpod, because students can download interactive presentations as homework, progress through the material at their own pace, and even take quizzes. Similar to the synchronous sessions, quiz results are automatically reported back to the professor from the field when the student's device connects to WiFi. And if you upgrade the app, students have the option to take notes on their device as they view the presentation in or out of class. Their own notes can be emailed back to them after the instructor views them."

If you have dipped your toes into the flipped classroom waters, consider how Nearpod and the techniques Yaros describe could generate engagement in your course.

Reprinted from *Online Classroom*, August 2015.

Improve Student Performance with Learning Logs

by John Orlando, Northcentral University

It is easy to forget that learning is not a simple transfer of information from the head of the teacher to the head of the student. Students build knowledge in their own heads through a combination of external cues and reflection. This reflection component is critical to moving information from working memory to long-term memory. In order to retain what we learn, we have to periodically reflect on the learning itself.

Kadriye O. Lewis, professor of pediatrics at the UKMC School of Medicine, uses learning logs to facilitate student reflection in her online courses. Learning logs are short journals that the students fill out after each lesson module to record what they have learned and their thoughts on the learning. Students respond to a number of question prompts, including:

- The amount of time I spent on different activities (readings, discussion, assignments) is…
- This week I studied…
- This week I learned…
- My difficulties are…
- I would like to know more about…
- I would like help with…
- My learning and practicing plans are…
- My reflection about the discussion topics is…
- My overall reflection on this week is…

These learning logs help the student process what he or she has learned in order to improve retention. They also improve the students' metacognitive ability to self-monitor their own learning, which has been proven to improve learning itself. Plus, they help students become more active learners by thinking about what they are getting out of the material as they go through it. Finally, they help the students become deeper thinkers as they practice reflecting on the underlying themes and meaning of class content and topics.

These learning logs also provide the teacher with valuable insights into the students. First, they help the teacher get to know the students. Most student/faculty interaction in an online environment is mediated by assignments. There is little interaction outside assessed requirements to help the teacher learn about the student himself or herself. The learning logs fill this gap with information about the student as a person.

Second, they express the instructor's interest in the student's learning, thus fostering rapport to improve the learning environment.

Third, they help the teacher discern what students are picking up and where they are struggling. It can be interesting to discover how students interpret the material and what they find important. Often students pick up different messages from the material than the instructor expects.

These logs allow the teacher to go back over the material in a different way, or to make revisions for the future.

Reprinted from *Online Classroom, December 2015.*

How Can I Keep Students Engaged with Instructor Presence?

by Deidre Price, Northwest Florida State College

Instructor presence is a popular topic, but perhaps one that seems too theoretical at times. Another way of thinking about this topic is: How can instructors be more human?

Online education provides students with greater access to information and education. It also provides them with greater agency, as it's a democratized space. Students are more likely to have their voices heard in an online classroom than they are in a face-to-face space. They also have greater continuity in the learning process, because it's available for them 24/7.

A lesser-known possibility of online education is that it can be as engaging and personable as the traditional classroom, a fact made possible through faculty presence. This is an element that's often overlooked and underestimated by faculty. But it's very definitely noticed by students. And it's often a determining factor for their success and overall satisfaction in a course.

There are two things to look out for when teaching an online class for the first time: 1) the symptoms of the absent professor, and 2) the symptoms of the robot professor.

The absent professor might have really good intentions and even a great course design. But that instructor might not seem like he or she is actually, physically there in the online classroom. An example of this would be a classroom that acts as a pass-through for publisher content. There might be one link provided at the start of the semester, and then students are expected to go to the publisher content and complete the assessments. Those assessments are auto-graded and then put back in the LMS. There isn't even really an illusion that there's a real professor out there, who's in an office waiting to help students.

Then we have the robot professor, who sends auto-generated email messages in 10-point font, using very sterile or overly technical writing. This can be off-putting for students, even though it might seem like it's very academic and professional from the instructor's perspective.

Either of these, the absent professor or the robot professor, can lead to higher attrition rates, lower grades, or academic dishonesty, since the students may not feel personally connected to the instructor or the class. No one might notice if a student even goes missing entirely. Community is certainly harder won in an online environment.

This could lead to a personal disconnect for students as well. One of the things that's really important to notice about instructor presence is that it influences the ways that our students interact with the course content, and also how they interact with the instructor. If you're not there, why should they be?

Reach out early

Overall, students often think of online instructors as not being real or as being absent, or think that they don't care. One way to overcome this myth is to reach out to students before the semester begins.

It may be a week or two before the semester starts, but students already have questions about the textbook or the class: "What is the syllabus? What do I start with? I want to get started now. How do I get hold of you? I'd like to come by and ask some questions about the class."

By reaching out to students first, before the semester begins, instructors can head off a lot of those questions. Then, once the course starts, a personal welcome email outside of the course and a welcome message posted inside the course will give students direction.

Tone is important. It's not enough just to send messages. Communication needs to be real, authentic, and positive. Which isn't to say an instructor is a "softball" professor, or someone who's just going to be an easy "A." Instead, what it means is that the instructor is available, accessible, and willing to work with students to make sure they're getting through the course successfully.

In communications, a signature with a picture allows students to connect a name with a face. Encourage students to also post pictures in the online classroom, as part of their profiles, to encourage an "e-meet." These need not be photos of themselves, however; it could be and avatar, or anything that reflects the student's personality.

First day

Ensure that your online classes are set up in a sensible order. Include a link on the front page of each class that shows students where to start. When students click on that button, they can navigate to everything they might need for class. Without that link, some students don't know that they need to go to the course content. Make this as clear as possible.

Include a welcome message that officially announces the start of class and invites students to the online classroom, so there is no confusion about when to start working through the course content. It's important to make sure that you take that extra step to reach out and make sure students feel welcome.

Providing clear navigation and instructions along the way, letting students know they can reach out if they need help—those extra little touches go a long way to helping students engage and learn.

When designing the class, think in terms of pictures and sounds. Make it feel real. Avoid clip art and use really good graphics. If it is clear that the instructor cares about the class, students will care more, too.

Include a common area for students to have some informal conversations. Think in terms of how students interact before and after class. These types of conversations typically don't have any place in the online classroom, unless an instructor establishes a space for them. So a commons area, a lobby, or even some kind of open discussion forum is a really great strategy for making sure your students can connect with each other and not feel isolated.

Feedback

Collective feedback, sent at regular intervals to the class as a whole regarding their progress, can be immensely helpful. Provide feedback that's not just personalized for each student, but that taps the trends that will allow students to know how the class as a whole is doing.

Following up with individual students outside of regular grading can also be helpful. If a student seems to be struggling or is absent from class, there are many things an instructor can do to reach out. The important thing is to do so early enough that the message can still be positive and hopeful, so that students don't feel as if their efforts are futile.

If a student isn't doing well, check in on them. Regular check-ins on student progress allows instructors to intervene quickly. If a student is absent, struggling, or failing, a personal message will be welcome. Another option is using intelligent agents. This speeds up the process and allows instructors to intervene at a really useful time. Offering ways for students to get back on track, showing students that they really do still have options—it's all part of going beyond the grade.

Go beyond the grade

Number grades are great, and students care about them, but explanation and personalized feedback that goes beyond the grade will allow students to grow and keep them engaged. Rerouting students back to content sections in assessment feedback will keep them invested in the classroom while encouraging the process of revisiting old course content so that students can brush up on the areas they're weak in and then do better for the long haul.

Communication is key. Make sure you're transparent. Be authentic. And admit when something needs attention. No news is never good news in an online classroom; it's a reason that some students start to panic.

How does the course content connect with life outside the classroom? Instructors seem more real when they connect their course content to what is going on in the world. If something relevant is happening in the news, an instructor can mention it in the online classroom. If he or she is planning to attend a conference that relates to the class, students might be interested in knowing about it. They want to see that their teacher is engaged with the world, not just with the class.

Students want to get to know their instructor, learning whether he or she has a reasonable sense of humor, and whether the instructor is an authentic person. With all this in mind, the sporadic and organic elements of the face-to-face class can finally be replicated within the online classroom.

Final interactions

Offering a recap or a formal goodbye to students at the end of a class is standard in a typical face-to-face class, and it's important to sum up what you've learned together at the end of the online class as well, such as in a goodbye post. This is a way for students to say goodbye to each other and to the instructor. Hopefully by now, students have formed some kind of meaningful learning community and these final interactions can be really powerful.

Being flexible and adjusting the course based on the feedback from real people taking it shows students once again that the instructor cares. Asking how students liked the course and what they would like to see next time shows that the instructor is truly interested and invested in them and the subject matter. The more human the instructor, the more invested the student.

Adapted from the Magna 20 Minute Mentor presentation, *How Can I Keep Students Engaged with Instructor Presence?*

Create Student Engagement with Your Videos

by John Orlando, Northcentral University

The traditional online course structure violates a fundamental principle of learning by separating the process of getting information from the process of engaging with it. The student is asked to go through some sort of resource in its entirety—be it a video, website, or reading—and then reflect on it later with an essay or discussion post.

The problem is that our working memory only holds a limited amount of information, and so we need to periodically pause what we are doing to reflect on the information in order to move it to our long-term memory. Without that engagement, much of what a student reads or views is forgotten by the time he or she gets to the assignment or discussion. The ideal learning environment requires students to engage with the content while they are receiving it.

One good way to reunite content and reflection is by adding tags to videos that pause them for the student to do something related to the content. If the video is on the structural dynamics of bridges, the instructor can add a tag that takes the student to a YouTube clip of the Tacoma bridge collapse. Not only does this new content reinforce and amplify the information in the original video, but the mere fact that the student has to act during the video helps keep his or her attention on the content, thus helping to impress the content into memory. These breaks take viewers out of the passive recipient role to become more active participants in their learning.

ThinkLink is one of my favorite sites for adding content to videos because it allows for easy upload and uses an intuitive tagging system. You can also upload images to ThinkLink for tagging. An art history professor might upload an image of a painting and add tags that elaborate on different elements within it. A tag on a building might explain its importance, history, or the style that it represents. Tagging allows the student to explore the content at his or her own pace and according to interest, which makes the learning self-directed rather than instructor-directed. Students' inquiries are directed by the question, "What is this?" when they click the tag, and so they are already invested in the answer.

Another way to create engagement is with periodic questions. These should come every 5 to 10 minutes, which is about the point when our minds start to wander. Even a very simple multiple-choice question about what the student just watched will do wonders for retention. Questions can even be humorous, including nonsense options among the possible answers, in order to keep the student's attention. They can also force students to apply what they're learning. After a discussion of John Locke, a philosophy professor might provide a list of objects and ask which ones Locke would consider to be examples of a "secondary quality." This forces the students to think about the content, thus better cementing it into their long-term memory.

There are a variety of good systems for adding questions to videos. Blubbr.tv allows you to create quizzes around YouTube videos. You can pick a video already on YouTube or load one that you create to your own YouTube account. The quizzes include a countdown timer to prevent lollygagging and to create anticipation. Students are told immediately whether they got the correct answer, and are given a running score as they move through the video.

PlayPosit is another popular choice for adding questions to videos. This tool differs from Blubbr.tv in that PlayPosit allows you to organize groups of videos into lessons, and then assign the lessons to students and track their progress through them. Students need to answer each question in a video before moving to the next, and since you are given the results, you can ensure that students do the entire lesson.

Student comments are a third way to create engagement with content. These allow students to post a thought when it occurs to them, rather than later in a discussion forum, when it has likely been forgotten. By being connected directly to the place where it is relevant, the comment gains context for other students. Plus, discussion forums tend to be driven by pre-established questions from the instructor, whereas an open video forum provides students with the freedom to add thoughts on the issues that come to mind, thus widening the creativity and breadth of the discussion. The instructor can also seed the forum by adding his or her own questions at different points to spark debate.

VideoNot.es is one of the better tools for adding comments to videos. Students watch the video and may stop it to add a note wherever appropriate. VideoNot.es is also integrated with Google Drive, meaning that students can save their notes directly to their Drive accounts to access, edit, or submit to their instructor later. Plus, the notes are time-stamped, so the instructor knows when they were posted, and can ensure that they were posted on time.

Vialogues is another good system for hosting video discussions, as it allows you to change up the interaction by alternating comments and polling questions in the video. You can even allow students to add their own polling questions, and so you might assign students to add questions at various points along the way. This is a fun exercise that forces students to pay attention, and the videos can be made either public or private to prevent non-students from messing with them. You can also embed the results into a blog or other website.

Create engagement with your learning content through video tags, comments, and questions, and see the difference it makes to student learning.

Reprinted from *Online Classroom,* December 2015.

Promoting Meaningful Engagement

by Stefan Perun, Villanova University

Live sessions in an online course create dynamic exchanges that lower students' anxiety about their learning by connecting them with their professor, classmates, and institution. They also enrich students' learning by giving them the space to think through ideas and encouraging them to reflect critically upon the course content and the perspectives of others.

However, live sessions also present challenges. The lack of physical presence makes it easy for students to multitask by doing something else during these sessions. And students don't want to be wrong, ask a "stupid" question, or otherwise embarrass themselves. Consequently, for students, the stakes are high: risk embarrassment to earn a good grade.

The challenge is to provide an experience that will engage students and meaningfully share information within the limits of the technology. John Immerwahr's (1994) framework of four Socratic questions—free fire, toss-up, inviter, and hot seat—is highly effective in meeting this challenge. The question types range from low to high stakes and can be used in combination to first get students participating and then move them to engaging in higher-level critical thinking.

Free Fire

The lowest stakes question type is the free fire. It is a prompt that any student can answer, as there are many answers, or any honest answer is acceptable. The instructor might ask students for their reaction to an author's argument or to a provocative statement by the instructor. This ultra-low-risk dynamic is a great icebreaker to get students active in a class discussion. But this question type does not necessarily require preparation or critical thinking, and thus is more likely to promote quantity, not quality, of answers.

Toss-up

A slightly higher stakes variation is the toss-up, a question to which there *is* a right answer, but anyone may respond (making it a good chat board or poll question). For example, the professor might ask, "What was the author's thesis statement?" This question type can also be a good discussion starter. The added advantage is everyone pauses on a key idea from an assigned reading or other source.

Compared to the free fire, the toss-up saves time by getting to the topic at hand quickly, and holds students more accountable for preparation. Given the higher stakes, there is a risk of receiving no response (after all, students do not like to be wrong). If the professor asks a toss-up and gets silence, then he or she can ask a more general free fire question to uncover the idea. Neither the free fire nor the toss-up promotes critical thinking; that can best be achieved with higher-stakes questions.

Inviter

After building participation, the professor can then shape a higher-level discussion with the inviter or hot seat question types. The inviter is a question to which there are many answers. For example, the professor might select a student who answered a toss-up correctly and invite him or her to explain "why" or "how."

This question type can force students to think more deeply about the course content. It is also interesting to students, and provides teachable moments. The professor might also use an inviter if he or she knows that a particular student has a good response. The professor might ask the student to elaborate upon a discussion board post or perhaps highlight salient points of a prior email exchange.

The inviter also brings risks. Inviting one student to respond to a follow-up question in front of the whole class puts that student on the spot. Inviting any student to respond to a question may result in that student simply talking about something with which he or she is comfortable and struggling to make connections to the ideas under study. This sets the stage for one student to monopolize the discussion, which can waste valuable time and/or require the professor to interrupt and refocus the student. In both cases, the inviter can create a confrontational feeling that might inadvertently promote hiding or diminish students' engagement in other areas of the course (e.g., discussion boards, emails, etc.).

The key to using the inviter productively is to give students an out by responding positively to whatever they say, especially if you interrupt them. In this way, the professor lowers the stakes of an otherwise high-stakes question, which mitigates the confrontational feel and encourages other students to take the risk of participating.

Hot seat

While lowering the stakes for students can equate to increased participation, consistently doing so can create a dynamic in which students do not feel the need to prepare. The highest-stakes question type—the hot seat—is needed as a follow-up (or a lead) to make the students uncomfortable enough to prepare, focus, and think critically. The professor asks one student a question to which there is only one right (or approximate) answer. The student must then think critically about the course content and how to use it to respond to the question. The professor will quickly identify to what extent a student has prepared and/or is paying attention, and other students will learn that everyone is accountable for preparation and substantive participation.

Remember, asking a student to respond on the spot is confrontational. The whole class will hear the student's understanding of the material and thinking process; the stakes are high for the student to save face. To manage this risk of diminishing participation, let students off the hook if they are wrong. Affirm a student's efforts with a statement like "You're almost there," and then change the question type to a toss-up by asking the class, "Who can help answer the question?"

Promoting meaningful engagement in the live virtual classroom is a matter of lowering the awkwardness and raising the stakes, and is well worth the effort to do so.

Reference

Immerwahr, J. "The Socratic Classroom: Classroom Communication Strategies." *Journal of Management Systems,* 6, no. 1 (1994): 37–44.

Reprinted from *Online Classroom,* January 2016.

Generating Lively Online Discussion

by John Orlando, Northcentral University

Discussion is a critical component of any online course, but instructors are often puzzled about what makes some discussions lively and others dead. To fill this gap, He and Gunter (2015) examined the factors that lead to participation in virtual teams and came up with some principles that can help guide instructors in cultivating a robust discussion in online courses.

Reputation

People will share knowledge with others when it enhances their reputation. It is easy to forget that students who speak in class are speaking not only to the instructor but to their classmates as well. They are cognizant of how they appear to their peers. Thus, they are less likely to take risks when there is an opportunity to be wrong in front of others.

So instead of asking questions with objective answers that can be wrong, with a particular answer in mind, it is better to ask questions that allow students to express and defend their own views. In particular, questions that allow students to bring in their own experiences to illustrate a point provide an easy way to contribute without fear of being wrong.

Replies

Students are more likely to get involved in a discussion when they think someone is reading comments, and replies are a measure of others' attention. Most online faculty require students to make one or more replies to other students in each forum, but they often forbid students to make simple "I agree" affirmations. While these signs of approval should not count toward a grade, there is no reason to forbid them. Just as we are encouraged by others liking our Facebook posts, students are encouraged by seeing other students approve of their posts, whether or not they are simple affirmations, so these signs of approval should not be discouraged.

Activity

Students are more likely to get involved in a discussion that is already active. Prior activity gives students more ideas for their own posts and demonstrates that others consider the topic interesting, which influences students' own perceptions of how interesting the discussion is. One good way to preserve activity is to space out postings. Students might be required to make an initial posting on Monday or Tuesday and then reply on Wednesday or Thursday. The instructor can also set a regular schedule for adding his or her own comments. This gives students a reason to periodically check in to get the latest updates.

Emotional bonds

Students are more comfortable participating when they feel an emotional bond of trust and comfort with others. This is what distinguishes productive discussions in an online course from the "flaming" posts on YouTube videos. The instructor can facilitate this bonding by requiring students to post a bio at the beginning of the course, and the instructor should take the lead by providing a bio for himself or herself. Students and instructors alike should be encouraged to make video bios—either using a webcam shot or the "digital storytelling" format of narration over imagery—that better humanize them to others.

Task conflict

A discussion in which everyone is just repeating what others say in different words is not interesting. Faculty should facilitate "task conflict," meaning disagreement about the task (not a personal disagreement) in order to generate interest. A discussion question might ask for positions on a controversial issue, one that allows for reasonable stances on either side. Of course, the instructor needs to monitor the discussion to make sure that it does not slip into personal attacks, but fortunately, this is rarely a problem in online courses. A boring discussion is more common than one with too much heat.

Leadership

While faculty normally set a minimum for participation, some people will naturally go beyond that and become leaders in the discussion. This is not a bad thing. These leaders can help seed the discussion with new ideas, and a group without leadership will have trouble getting going.

The trick is to avoid having these leaders monopolize debate and thus quash activity by others. Because there is no time limit to discussion online, as there is in a face-to-face course, one person's posting does not prevent others from making posts. But too many postings by one person can create the impression of an unbalanced discussion. This can happen when one person seems compelled to reply to all others. Talk to anyone who seems to be monopolizing discussions, but understand that any group needs leaders, and so allow people to take leadership roles that help provide the nudge that gets discussion going. You can even reach out to individual students to ask them to take the lead on certain discussions, as a coach does with particular players. Students will generally feel complimented and respond positively when this happens.

Following these few simple principles will lead to exciting discussion in any online class.

Reference

He, J., and G. Gunter. "Examining Factors That Affect Students' Knowledge Sharing within Virtual Teams." *Journal of Interactive Learning Research* 26, no. 2 (2015): 169–87.

Reprinted from *Online Classroom*, January 2016.

Continuous Assessments for Better Learning

by John Orlando, Northcentral University

We tend to think of assessments solely as devices for measuring learning. But they also influence *how* students learn, because students tailor their study strategies to their assessments. This means that you need to think of your assessments as teaching devices themselves.

Naomi Holmes at the University of Northampton tested how assessments influenced learning by comparing learning outcomes and student preferences for a single online assessment at the end of a geography course to short online assessments given weekly during the course. The short assessments were mostly multiple-choice questions, though they sometimes involved short answers. Soon after submitting a weekly quiz, students were also given feedback on whether they had answered questions correctly and why.

One major outcome of the study was that students given weekly tests showed improved grades compared to their single-test peers. The percentage of students achieving the equivalent of a first-class or upper-second-class grade in the module went from 54 percent to 63 percent. As a result, a whopping 82 percent of students preferred the weekly tests, while only 6 percent preferred the term test, with 94 percent of students believing that the weekly quiz format improved their learning.

Students opined about the various ways that the continuous assessments improved their learning. A common view was that the quizzes improved students' study habits by helping them structure their study. The single assessment at the end of the term allowed students to put off studying to the indefinite future, causing them to lose much of the information that they were given in lectures and readings. Students who were given weekly quizzes were focused on keeping up with material during the course.

Students who took weekly quizzes also showed a marked improvement in their lecture attendance, with the number of students attending all lectures going up from 8 percent to 59 percent. Plus, students taking weekly quizzes were far more likely to review their notes after a lecture. This after-lecture review was critical to learning and was something that most students did not consider when the assessment was not looming on the horizon. Some students also said that the quizzes led to spending more time studying overall.

Another finding was that students found the quizzes more stimulating and engaging than the end-of-term assessment. This led them to be more focused during the assessments and to pay more attention to making sure they understood what was taught. It also gave them the feeling of building their knowledge base each week.

Finally, the immediate feedback provided by the weekly assessments allowed students to check their understanding of the material immediately after being introduced to it, which provided them with opportunities to correct any misunderstandings. The feedback also showed them where they were studying incorrectly or inefficiently, allowing them to revise their study habits as they went along. This meant that students could better prepare for the next quiz, which lowered their overall stress when taking the assessments.

It is easy to set up auto-graded quizzes in online courses. While there are many good reasons for including large assessments such as research papers and projects in a course, this study shows that the online instructor can improve learning outcomes by adding short, frequent assessments throughout the course.

Reference

Holmes, Naomi. "Student Perceptions of Their Learning and Engagement in Response to the Use of a Continuous E-Assessment in an Undergraduate Module." *Assessment & Evaluation in Higher Education* 40, no. 1 (2015): 1–14.

Reprinted from *Online Classroom,* June 2016.

Five Tips to Engage Students Outside of the Online Classroom

by Stephanie Delaney, Seattle Central Community College

Ubiquitous learning—the idea that everywhere you go, you're learning all the time—lets us take advantage of the concept that in every interaction, there may be opportunities for students to engage with our subject matter, if we can just get them into that holistic thinking mode.

I am an avid knitter and like to knit all the time. When I need to learn something new about knitting, I'll often go to YouTube or to some other online videos that I've seen. I might read a book or take an online course to learn some new ideas. I might talk with others who I see knitting or people who approach me. I like to knit out in public so that people might come up to me and talk about what I'm knitting.

Searching the web, talking with others, trial and error—these are good ways to learn things through experimentation and trying things out. But how does one get into this holistic thinking mindset in the classroom?

Student polling

I have done student polling in my American government class. And I've asked students to go out and ask people, "If you could change one of your constitutional rights, what would that be? Would you add a right? Would you get rid of a right? Would you amend a right? How would you change it and what would the result be?"

This accomplishes all sorts of things. First, students have to understand what their constitutional rights are. In particular, they have to understand their First Amendment rights and then, inevitably, they have to be able to explain them to other students, because the people they talk to often don't know what their First Amendment rights are, let alone their other constitutional rights. And it gets students into some conversations about what these rights are and what they might change, what people like and don't like, and what's really there and what's not there—what people thought they had a right to but don't really.

So this is a great technique to get students to interact with this concept in a way that they wouldn't by just reading a chapter. They take the question out to their home, to their relatives, to their children, to their classmates in other courses. Sometimes they'll post the questions on social media. Sometimes they'll ask their peers at work. There are all sorts of ways in which go out and ask that question, and it inevitably generates discussion. I always require students to talk to at least 10 people. And so that really gives them 10 dialogues about their constitutional rights. By the time they bring the information from their poll back to their classmates, they really know all about this concept and really internalize the depth of understanding, or lack thereof, in the community about these issues.

It's a fun and engaging activity for students. They really enjoy it. It's particularly great for first-generation students who've never been to college before and whose family members have not been to college. These individuals may not understand what this person does all day at school. So being able to bring conversations like this home is just really wonderful for those students.

Now, how do they bring it back? One of the easiest ways is simply to use the discussion tool in any learning management system (LMS). That's what I generally do. I have students go out, ask the question, and then summarize the results, perhaps highlighting the most interesting or most surprising result and then sharing the results back with the class or with a small group of their peers. Students can share those results on the discussion board or talk in small groups. If it's a hybrid class, this might be a jumping-off point for a conversation in the face-to-face classroom after they've done this engagement activity outside in the community. There are all sorts of ways that students can bring that polling back into the classroom.

Student interviews

Student interviews allow students an opportunity to interview someone out in the community. You might have students do this using video or audio, then ask them to share those results back with the class. Arranging a course-relevant person for the student to interview is important. For example, in a political science class, students might find a community activist, someone who is ideally active in a topic that is interesting to the students, and talk to them about what it's like to be a community activist, how they got started, what they do to create action, how to be an activist, and questions of that sort.

Once again, students bring those interviews back to the classroom. This is a great opportunity for students to make good use of their mobile devices, which most own, and those devices usually have recording features that allow them to record an interview using just audio or audio and video, or even record right into a learning management system. Students are often perfectly comfortable with these technologies and they're really happy to go out and do this assignment. If they're not entirely comfortable, it's relatively easy for them to learn how to use these technology tools. Students, when given the challenge, are able to go out and learn how to use the technologies available to them, even if they're asking their peers or talking to other people in the college for help. For fully online students who might feel a little bit more isolated, the campus technology center can serve as a resource, and I encourage students to visit if they need assistance.

Service learning

Service learning is one of those topics that people don't always consider in online classes. Online students don't expect to have to go somewhere else to do their coursework, especially during business hours when they may work or have other obligations. But some service learning projects don't require going somewhere out of the way during the day. Rather, a call-to-action project asks students to challenge people to do something related to the class and see whether they do it or not.

For example, in a comparative environmental studies class, students might challenge their workmates to recycle in the workplace or challenge their neighbors to recycle in an apartment complex. Students could challenge people to get energy-efficient light bulbs for their most frequently used lamp or lighting areas or encourage digital activism through signing petitions or making donations to a charitable cause.

In this exercise, students come up with the topic and the call to action—for example, change out 10 light bulbs in your home. Then they assign the challenge to personal contacts, neighbors, coworkers, or classmates. They might even use social media. (The one caveat here is that the 10 people must not all be immediate family members. Again, this is a community activity, and a student's immediate family is not the community.)

Picking their project is the first step. Second, students choose their audience, whether a workmate or a neighbor. Third, they choose the call to action. Students are encouraged to give their audience at least three weeks to complete the call to action, depending on how complex the task is—more if they can. Students might send out a reminder every week or so to their audience, which creates a more active, less passive, waiting period.

At the end, students follow up and find out whether the audience did what they were asked. If they didn't, why not? What prevented them from engaging in the call to action? Even if no one follows through on the call to action, as long as they took the appropriate steps, students can still get a good grade on this assignment. There are two takeaways from this assignment: one, it's hard to get people to change. People want to do what they've always been doing and calling on them to change can be a challenge. And two, one person *can* make a difference.

Take other classes

While we spend a lot of time thinking about our own class, it's really great for students to put their learning into context by picking other classes as a supplement. So where might this other class be? Students might take a massive open online course (MOOC)—these are free and customizable, and because it is not necessary to finish the courses, students can pick and choose what to focus on.

Students can also learn from YouTube or TED Talk videos, which helps them adopt lifelong learning habits and opens them up to follow the pathway of their interest related to their coursework. This generates excitement, as students tend to want to dig deeper when they're able to direct their learning in this way, and it's a great way to build enthusiasm about a class.

With this assignment, as with any assignment, making expectations clear is key. How much time should students spend? Giving them some context for these "alternative" assignments can be really helpful.

Home laboratory

In a home laboratory, students experiment with a theory and report their findings to the instructor or to the class. "Laboratory" tends to sound science-based, but there are many experiments students can do that are not necessarily science-related. For example, history students could search for something of historical significance near their home or along their commute.

A neat example that would work for a psychology class is to have students break an innocent social norm, like facing the back wall when they get into an elevator or facing the side wall—just doing something opposite of what is expected and then reporting on how people respond to that strange action.

And then of course, for the sciences, all sorts of home labs can be done with typical household products. (The Internet is full of ideas for different home labs.) Students are armed with the general steps and your expectations and then report back when they complete the experiment. The process gives them the opportunity to try several times and also gives room for failure.

That is another great way to learn: by having the freedom to fail. The opportunity for failure and the chance to learn from that failure is a fabulous thing for students. Expecting perfection with every activity can be incredibly stifling to students' creativity and willingness to learn something new. To get them to stretch beyond what they know, there must be room for failure. And home labs can really create that space for failure, and for trying again, without the fear of being punished by a bad grade.

Giving students authority to be creative and to contextualize learning to their own lives, based on what's interesting to them, makes the whole class more lively and engaging. It also gives instructors the opportunity to get to know students a different way, to get to know a little bit about their lives and their backgrounds as they share their selections in these types of assignments.

These assignments create community in the class, and that kind of community building really creates better retention. Students want to stay in classes where they feel like they're part of the community. It creates a sense of caring. When an instructor creates activities like this, students feel cared for. And students tend to stay in classes where they feel like the instructor cares about them. These are all sorts of great reasons to do these types of nonstandard activities.

Grading

The aforementioned types of activities are likely new to students, which can cause anxiety. Keeping assignment instructions and expectations clear is important. If the goal is simply to get students thinking and talking, tell them that so they know just what you're looking for and where they should focus their effort. Give them the rubric up front and tell them, "Here's how you're going to be graded." I also encourage complete/incomplete grading, so even if students do the assignments by simply following the steps, they'll get full credit. If they don't do the work, they won't get the grade.

It's important, too, to keep in mind that these types of assignments may, at first, be quite fear-inducing and stressful for students. These may not be ideal assignments for the week of class, but consider implementing such engaging assignments further down the road, once a trust relationship has been built between instructor and student.

Adapted from the Magna Online Seminar presentation, *Five Tips to Engage Students Outside of the Online Classroom.*

About the Contributors

Stephanie Delaney is the dean of the center for extended learning at Seattle Central Community College. There, she supports faculty in eLearning pedagogy and supports students in learning successfully online. She also teaches online courses in law and the global environment. Delaney earned her PhD in educational leadership in higher education/distance education at the University of Nebraska at Lincoln.

Oliver Dreon is an associate professor in the School of Education at Millersville University of Pennsylvania. He teaches a wide variety of education and instructional technology courses in both face-to-face and online formats, and also coordinates the university's Digital Learning Studio. He is the coauthor of the book *Authentic Instruction with Technology: A Student-Centered Approach* and has published in various journals, including the *Middle Level Journal, TechTrends,* and *Teachers and Teaching.*

Steve Dwinnells is director of the e-Campus Instructional Development Center at Eastern Kentucky University.

Alisha Etheredge is an adjunct professor of chemistry at Strayer University.

Lynn Gillette is the provost and vice president of academic affairs at Nicholls State University. He is also the former president of Sierra Nevada College in Incline Village, Nevada. During his time as provost and president, he led the college to unprecedented financial stability, increased retention and graduation rates, and increased undergraduate enrollment to record highs.

Dr. J. Robert Gillette joined the faculty at the University of Kentucky in 1994 and is an associate professor of economics. Before coming to UK, he taught at Texas A&M University and Washington State University and worked with an economic consulting firm. Dr. Gillette has authored or co-authored economic studies for various public agencies, including the Internal Revenue Service and the State of California, and for numerous private organizations.

Tyler Griffin is an assistant professor at Brigham Young University. With degrees in electrical engineering and instructional technology, combined with 18 years of professional teaching experience, he teaches more than 1,000 students per semester and loves how technology can help to "shrink" large classrooms. Griffin is also actively involved in designing and developing 3-D immersive learning environments for his students.

Gary R. Hafer is the John P. Graham Teaching Professor at Lycoming College in Williamsport, Pennsylvania, where he teaches writing to undergraduates in all disciplines. His short studies on writing instruction have appeared in *College English, The Journal of Developmental Education*, and *Computers and Composition*. In addition, Hafer is production design editor for *Brilliant Corners*, the only journal devoted to jazz and literature.

Amy Hankins has worked in education for 10 years, including online learning for eight years. Currently she is working as a full-time instructor for an online university.

Jessica Harris is a librarian at Santa Rosa Junior College in Santa Rosa, California, and the former director of research services at Bain Capital.

Robert (Rob) Kelly is former editor of the *Academic Leader* and *Online Classroom* newsletters and assisted with *The Teaching Professor* newsletter for Magna Publications. Rob has a BA in political science/liberal arts from the College of New Jersey and studied journalism at West Virginia University.

Dr. Poonam Kumar is the director of online/hybrid learning at Saginaw Valley State University.

Sami Lange is a full-time librarian and instructor at Santa Rosa Junior College, Petaluma, California.

Jennifer Patterson Lorenzetti is managing editor of *Academic Leader: The Newsletter for Academic Deans and Department Chairs*. She is a writer, speaker, higher education consultant, and the owner of Hilltop Communications. She has worked in and written about higher education for more than 20 years, and is the author of *Lecture Is Not Dead: Ten Tips for Delivering Dynamic Lectures in the College Classroom.*

Jean Mandernach's research focuses on enhancing student learning through assessment and innovative online instructional strategies. Jean received her BS in comprehensive psychology from the University of Nebraska at Kearney, an MS in experimental psychology from Western Illinois University, and a PhD in social psychology from the University of Nebraska at Lincoln.

Diane Monsivais is an assistant professor/advisor for the MSN in nursing education at the University of Texas at El Paso.

Cheryl Murphy is associate professor of educational technology at the University of Arkansas.

John Orlando helped build and direct distance learning programs at the University of Vermont and Norwich University, and has written more than 50 articles and delivered more than 40 presentations and keynotes on teaching with technology, online education, and social media. He is the associate director of the Faculty Resource Center at Northcentral University. He is also the editor of *Online Classroom.*

Stephan Perun is an assistant professor of public administration at Villanova University.

Deidre Price specializes in teaching online and hybrid writing courses at Northwest Florida State College, where she has served as professor of English for the past 12 years and where she has chaired the distance learning and technology committees. She has had numerous speaking engagements at various national English and information literacy conferences on the subject of technology and online communication, specifically related to social media, blog culture, and best practices in the online classroom.

Robert Prince is an associate professor of journalism at the University of Alaska Fairbanks and host of the radio program and podcast "Dark Winter Nights: True Stories from Alaska," which is available on iTunes or at *darkwinternights.com.*

Jill Schiefelbein is a speaker, author, award-winning entrepreneur, and no stranger to the higher education environment. She worked in multiple levels of academia over an 11-year period, including holding positions as a lecturer, faculty, director, and administrator. Schiefelbein is coauthor of *Business and Professional Communication in the Global Workplace*, a frequent guest on business podcasts, and an official video partner and contributing writer for *Entrepreneur*.

Dr. Marilyn Skrocki is an associate professor of health sciences at Saginaw Valley State University.

Tom Tobin is the coordinator of learning technologies at the Center for Teaching and Learning at Northeastern Illinois University. His work focuses on using technology to extend the reach of higher education beyond its traditional audience. He advocates for the educational rights of people with disabilities and people from disadvantaged backgrounds.

Maryellen Weimer has been the guiding hand and constant voice behind *The Teaching Professor* newsletter since 1987. She is an award-winning professor emerita of teaching and learning at Penn State Berks and won Penn State's Milton S. Eisenhower award for distinguished teaching in 2005. She has published several books, including *Inspired College Teaching: A Career-Long Resource for Professional Growth* (Jossey-Bass, 2010).

Ronald A. Yaros is associate professor of journalism at the University of Maryland–College Park.

Suzanne Zak is an EdDCT candidate in music and music education at Teachers College, Columbia University.

Rebecca Zambrano is the director of online faculty development at Edgewood College in Madison, Wisconsin, where she has created, developed, and taught on-ground, blended, and online courses in the School of Education since 2004.

Additional Resources

If you enjoyed this book, Magna Publications has additional resources for you:

BULK PURCHASES

To purchase multiple print copies of this book, please visit: www.MagnaGroupBooks.com

BOOKS

Essential Teaching Principles:
A Resource Collection for Adjunct Faculty
https://www.amazon.com/dp/B01HSEC0V2
This book provides a wealth of both research-driven and classroom-tested best practices to help adjuncts develop the knowledge and skills required to run a successful classroom.

Teaching Strategies for the College Classroom:
A Collection of Faculty Articles
http://amzn.to/Yas3NE
Practical, classroom-tested "tool kit" for faculty members who would like to develop their teaching practice. Contains concrete pedagogical strategies that have been tested in the authors' classrooms and together form a handbook of classroom strategies.

Grading Strategies for the College Classroom:
A Collection of Articles for Faculty
http://amzn.to/15RhFLX
This book provides insights into managing the complicated task of assigning a simple letter to a semester's work. It's a must-read for any faculty member seeking to understand how to use assessment to measure and enhance performance.

SUBSCRIPTIONS

Faculty Focus
www.facultyfocus.com
A free e-newsletter on effective teaching strategies for the college classroom, featuring a weekly blog post from Maryellen Weimer, PhD.

The Teaching Professor Newsletter
www.TeachingProfessorNewsletter.com
Published ten times a year, *The Teaching Professor* features ideas, insights, and best pedagogical practices written for and by educators who are passionate about teaching. Edited by Maryellen Weimer, PhD.

Online Classroom Newsletter
www.OnlineClassroomNewsletter.com
Published twelve times a year, *Online Classroom* helps you understand the current trends, challenges, ideas, and pedagogical insights for effective online instruction. Edited by John Orlando, PhD.

20-Minute Mentor Commons
http://bit.ly/2biCIR3
20-Minute Mentor Commons gives your entire campus unlimited, on-demand access to a library of Magna 20-Minute Mentor programs. This resource continues to grow as more programs are added regularly. They feature the top experts in higher education ready to answer pressing questions whenever, and wherever, your faculty need answers.

CONFERENCES

The Teaching Professor Conference
www.TeachingProfessor.com
This annual event provides an opportunity to learn effective pedagogical techniques, hear from leading teaching experts, and interact with colleagues committed to teaching and learning excellence.

The Teaching Professor Technology Conference
www.TeachingProfessorTechnologyConference.com
This conference examines the technologies that are changing the way teachers teach and students learn, while giving special emphasis to the pedagogically effective ways you can harness these new technologies in your courses and on your campus.

44109355R00094

Made in the USA
Middletown, DE
29 May 2017